CONFESSION OF FAITH

and

GOVERNMENT

of the

Cumberland Presbyterian Church
Cumberland Presbyterian Church in America

1984

Approved June 1984
by
THE GENERAL ASSEMBLIES

August 2024 Printing

Published by
THE OFFICE OF THE GENERAL ASSEMBLY

8207 Traditional Place
Cordova, TN 38016

August 2024 Edition
Fourteenth Edition, First Printing

This edition of the *Confession of Faith* includes all amendments to the *Confession* and the *Constitution* made to and including the year 2024.

Printed in the United States of America

Additional copies available from:

Cumberland Presbyterian Resource Center
8207 Traditional Place
Cordova, TN 38016
1-901-276-4572 ext 252

PREFACE TO THE 1883 CONFESSION

The Cumberland Presbyterian Church was organized in Dickson County, Tennessee, February 4, A.D. 1810. It was an outgrowth of the Great Revival of 1800--one of the most powerful revivals that this country has ever witnessed. The founders of the church were Finis Ewing, Samuel King, and Samuel McAdow. They were ministers in the Presbyterian Church, who rejected the doctrine of election and reprobation as taught in the Westminster Confession of Faith. The causes which led to the formation of the church are clearly and distinctly set forth in publications issued at the time, and in various tracts and books published subsequently. To these the reader is referred for full information on the subject.

The Cumberland Presbytery, which was constituted at the time of the organization of the church, and which originally consisted of only three ministers, was in three years sufficiently large to form three Presbyteries. These Presbyteries, in October, A.D. 1813, met at the Beech Church, in Sumner County, Tennessee, and constituted a Synod. This Synod at once formulated and published a "Brief Statement," setting forth the points wherein Cumberland Presbyterians dissented from the Westminster Confession of Faith. They are as follows:

1. That there are no eternal reprobates.

2. That Christ died not for a part only, but for all mankind.

3. That all infants dying in infancy are saved through Christ and the sanctification of the Spirit.

4. That the Spirit of God operates on the world, or as co-extensively as Christ has made atonement, in such a manner as to leave all men inexcusable.

At this same meeting of Synod, too, a committee was appointed to prepare a Confession of Faith. The next year, A. D. 1814, at Sugg's Creek Church, Wilson County, Tennessee, the report of the committee was presented to Synod, and the revision of the Westminster Confession of Faith which they presented was unanimously adopted as the Confession of Faith of the Cumberland Presbyterian Church. Subsequently the formation of the General Assembly took place. This judicature, at its first meeting, A.D. 1829, at Princeton, Kentucky, made such changes in the Form of Government as were demanded by the formation of this new court.

In compiling the Confession of Faith, the fathers of the

Cumberland Presbyterian Church had one leading thought before them, and that was to so modify the Westminster Confession as to eliminate therefrom the doctrine of universal fore-ordination and its legitimate sequences, unconditional election and reprobation, limited atonement, and divine influence correspondingly circumscribed. All the boldly-defined statements of the doctrine objected to were expunged, and corrected statements were made. But it was impossible to eliminate all the features of hyper-Calvinism from the Westminster Confession of Faith by simply expunging words, phrases, sentences, or even sections, and then attempting to fill the vacancies thus made by corrected statements or other declarations, for the objectionable doctrine, with its logical sequences, pervaded the whole system of theology formulated in that book.

The compilers knew this, and they also knew that a book thus made must necessarily have some defects. Still they felt assured that they had prepared one which could not be fairly and logically interpreted without contradicting the most objectionable features of hyper-Calvinism; and they felt, too, that they had formulated a system of doctrines which any candid inquirer after truth might understand. They did not, however, claim that the time would never come when there might be a demand for a restatement of these doctrines, which would set forth more clearly and logically the system of theology believed and taught by the Cumberland Presbyterian Church. That time did come, and so general was the desire throughout the church to have the Confession of Faith revised that at the General Assembly which convened in the city of Austin, Texas, A. D. 1881, a paper was introduced looking to that end, and it was adopted by a unanimous vote.

In view of the great importance of the work, two committees were appointed, and it was made the duty of the first committee to revise the Confession of Faith and Government, and of the second to review and revise the work of the first. The committees met at Lebanon, Tennessee, the seat of Cumberland University, where every facility could be enjoyed for such labors, having free access to a fine theological library. After bestowing great labor upon their work, giving every item earnest and prayerful attention, the committees completed the tasks assigned them, and the results of their labors were published in pamphlet form and in weekly papers of the church for information, "that criticism might be made by those desiring to do so." The committees, after receiving these criticisms, again met and remained in session for a number of days, giving careful and prayerful consideration to all the suggestions made. They then completed their work without a single dissent, and submitted the result to the General Assembly which convened in the city of Huntsville, Alabama, A.D. 1882. That General Assembly, in "Committee of the Whole," considered with great patience and care every item in the entire book, taking a vote on each one separately, and at the close of each chapter of subject taking a vote upon it as a whole. In this way the entire book, from beginning to end, was carefully and prayerfully scrutinized, and necessary changes were made--the most of them verbal; and there was not in the final vote a single negative!

Having completed its work, the General Assembly transmitted the book to the Presbyteries for their approval or disapproval. The reports from the Presbyteries to the next General Assembly, which convened in the city of Nashville, Tennessee, A.D. 1883, showed that this work had been almost unanimously adopted. The General Assembly, having reviewed these returns from the Presbyteries, formally declared said book to be the Confession of Faith and Government of the Cumberland Presbyterian Church.

The book is now sent forth with the strongest convictions that it is in accord with the word of God. Let it be tested, not by tradition, but by the Holy Scriptures, the only infallible rule of faith and practice.

The General Assembly, at Bentonville, Arkansas, A.D. 1885, ordered the insertion of the foregoing Preface without referring the same to the Presbyteries.

INTRODUCTION TO 1883 CONFESSION

1. God alone is Lord of the conscience, and has left it unfettered by the doctrines and commandments of men which are in any thing contrary to his word. The right of private judgment, therefore, in respect to religion, is universal and inalienable. No religious organization should be aided by the civil power further than may be necessary for protection, and this should be afforded to all alike.

2. Our Blessed Saviour, for the edification of the visible Church, has appointed officers not only to preach the gospel and to administer the sacraments, but also to exercise discipline; and it is incumbent upon these officers, and upon the whole church in whose name they act, to censure or suspend for the privileges of the church the disorderly, or to excommunicate the heretical and scandalous--observing in all cases the rules contained in the word of God.

3. No error can be more pernicious or more absurd than that which represents it as a matter of but little consequence what a man's opinions are; for there is an inseparable connection between faith and practice, truth and holiness; otherwise it would be of no consequence to discover truth or to embrace it. Our Saviour has said, "A corrupt tree cannot bring forth good fruit."

4. While it is necessary that all who are admitted as teachers should be sound in the faith, nevertheless there are doctrines and forms with respect to which men of good character and principles may differ; and in all these it is the duty of all private Christians and religious bodies to exercise forbearance toward one another.

5. Though the character, qualifications, and authority of church-officers are laid down in the Holy Scriptures, as well as the proper method of their investiture, yet the right to select the persons who shall exercise this authority, in any particular body, belongs to that body.

6. All church-power however exercised, is ministerial and declarative only; that is, the Holy Scriptures are the only infallible rule of faith and practice. No church-judicatory ought to assume, by virtue of its own authority, to make laws to bind the conscience; and all its decisions should be founded upon the revealed will of God. Ecclesiastical discipline is altogether distinct from the civil magistracy, and church-judicatories do not possess any civil jurisdiction--cannot inflict any civil penalties, nor have they any jurisdiction in political or civil affairs. Their power is wholly moral

and ecclesiastical. They possess the right of requiring obedience to the laws of Christ, may frame articles of faith, may bear testimony against error in doctrine and immorality in practice, and may exclude the disobedient and disorderly from the privileges of the church. They possess the power requisite for obtaining evidence and inflicting censure. They can call before them any offender against the order and government of the church. They can require members of their own body to appear and give testimony, and also introduce other witnesses when necessary. But the highest punishment to which their authority extends is to exclude the contumacious and impenitent from the communion and fellowship of the church.

7. Every Christian church, or union, or association of particular churches, has the right to declare the terms of admission into its communion, and the qualifications of its ministers, officers, and members as well as the whole system of its internal government.

In the exercise of this right, the Cumberland Presbyterian Church, adhering to the foregoing general principles, adopts the following as its system of faith and internal government, consisting: 1. Of the Confession of Faith. 2. Of the Catechism. 3. Of the Constitution. 4. Of the Rules of Discipline. 5. Of the General Regulations. 6. Of the Directory of Worship. 7. Of the Rules of Order.

PREFACE TO THE 1984 CONFESSION

In 1977 the One Hundred Forty-Seventh General Assembly of the Cumberland Presbyterian Church voted to initiate a revision of the *Confession of Faith* of 1883. The following year the One Hundred Forty-Eighth General Assembly appointed a committee of sixteen persons to implement the work of revision and the committee was given guidelines for its work. In addition to the committee to revise the *Confession of Faith*, the General Assembly appointed a panel of readers consisting of twenty persons to review the work of the committee and make suggestions before the proposed revision was submitted to the churches for study.

Recognizing that the *Confession of Faith* was used by both the Cumberland Presbyterian Church and the Second Cumberland Presbyterian Church, the Cumberland Presbyterian Church invited the Second Cumberland Presbyterian Church to participate in the revision. The One Hundred Fourth General Assembly of the Second Cumberland Presbyterian Church appointed five persons to the committee, and a panel of readers. From this point forward the work of revision was a joint effort of the two denominations. Each denomination appointed a co-chairperson from its committee membership.

The One Hundred Forty-Ninth General Assembly of the Cumberland Presbyterian Church and the One hundred Fifth General Assembly of the Second Cumberland Presbyterian Church adopted the principle that the proposed revision would require adoption by the general assemblies of both denominations before it would be sent to presbyteries for a vote of approval or disapproval.

The committee began its work by all its members studying and revising the doctrinal portion of the *Confession of Faith*. There were three primary objective references to guide the committee: (1) the Holy Scriptures, (2) the "Brief Statement" formulated in 1810 which contains the "four points" the founders of the church set forth as the departure from "hyper-Calvinism," (3) the articles of the *Confession of Faith* themselves. The articles of the 1883 Confession were, without exception, the beginning point in the formulation of the revision. In no case did the work of revision begin at some other point--as would have been the procedure had the general assemblies ordered the writing of an entirely new creed. Each article of the Confession of 1883 was tested by the Holy Scriptures, the historical context of the Church in 1883 and the present time, the development of the Church in general and the Cumberland Presbyterian Church in particular from 1810 to the present, and the language usage which was current in 1883 and is current in the present.

By July of 1980 the committee had made its initial revision of the *Confession of Faith,* and submitted its work to the panel of readers for criticism and suggestions. Subsequently, changes which reflected the critique of the panel of readers were made in the initial draft of the doctrinal statements. The same procedure was followed with the Constitution and the Rules of Discipline being referred to the panel of readers in December 1980.

The committee submitted to the general assemblies of 1981 its draft of the Confession, the Constitution, and the Rules of Discipline for study and response by the churches at large. Responses were received from study groups, sessions, presbyteries, and individuals. Subsequently, the committee again revised its work in the light of these responses as a mark of its intention that the *Confession of Faith* be the work of the entire church rather than that of a committee. A similar procedure was followed by the committee in its revision of the Directory for Worship and Rules of Order; these were submitted to the general assemblies in 1982 and, likewise, were accepted and referred to the churches for study and response.

By the Fall of 1982 the committee completed its work on the Confession, the Constitution, and the Rules of Discipline. In early 1983 it completed its work on the Directory for Worship and Rules of Order and submitted all these documents to the two general assemblies, which met concurrently in Birmingham, Alabama, in 1983. The two general assemblies met in joint session and heard the co-chairpersons of the Revision Committee make a presentation regarding the proposed revision. The general assemblies then reassembled, each in its own meeting place, and considered the work of the revision in a Committee of the Whole.

The General Assembly of the Cumberland Presbyterian Church approved the work of the revision, which included the revised Preface, Introduction, the Confession, the Constitution, the Rules of Discipline, the Directory for Worship, and the Rules of Order and, by a vote of 112 for and 9 against, sent the documents to its presbyteries for a vote of ratification.

The General Assembly of the Second Cumberland Presbyterian Church approved the work of revision which included the revised Preface, Introduction, the Confession, the Constitution, the Rules of

Discipline, the Directory for Worship, and the Rules of Orders and, by unanimous vote, sent the documents to its presbyteries for a vote for ratification.

The returns from the presbyteries of the Cumberland Presbyterian Church were reviewed by its General Assembly of 1984, meeting in Chattanooga, Tennessee, which declared the revised *Confession of Faith* to be adopted by the necessary three-fourths of the presbyteries voting affirmatively. The returns from the presbyteries of the Second Cumberland Presbyterian Church were reviewed by its General Assembly of 1984, meeting in Chattanooga, Tennessee, which declared the revised *Confession of Faith* to be adopted by the necessary three-fourths of its presbyteries voting affirmatively.

Each General Assembly formally declared the revision to be the *Confession of Faith* of the Cumberland Presbyterian Church and the Second Cumberland Presbyterian Church.

The Preface was updated by the Stated Clerks upon adoption of the Confession of Faith in 1984.

NOTE: In 1992 the name of the Second Cumberland Presbyterian Church was changed to Cumberland Presbyterian Church in America. This name change will be reflected in the pages that follow.

CONTENTS

PREFACE TO THE 1883 CONFESSION..iii

INTRODUCTION TO 1883 CONFESSION vi

PREFACE TO THE 1984 CONFESSION..viii

INTRODUCTION TO THE 1984 CONFESSION....................................... xv

CONFESSION OF FAITH
1.00   God Speaks to the Human Family... 1
       The Living God 1
       The Holy Scriptures... 1
       God's Will.. 2
       Creation 3
       Providence 3
       The Law of God 4
2.00   The Human Family Breaks Relationship With God............ 4
       Human Freedom.. 4
       The Abuse of Freedom 5
3.00   God Acts Through Jesus Christ to Reconcile the World 5
       God's Covenant 5
       Christ the Savior... 6
4.00   God Acts Through the Holy Spirit...................................... 7
       The Call and Work of the Holy Spirit 7
       Repentance and Confession.. 7
       Saving Faith.. 8
       Justification.. 8
       Regeneration and Adoption 9
       Sanctification and Growth in Grace 10
       Preservation of Believers... 10
       Christian Assurance 11
5.00   God Creates the Church for Mission 11
       The Church 11
       Christian Communion 12
       Christian Worship.. 13
       Sacraments... 13
       Baptism... 14
       The Lord's Supper 14
       The Church in Mission 15
       Church Government 15
       Church Judicatories 16
6.00   Christians Live and Witness in the World 16
       Christian Freedom 16
       Good Works.. 17
       Christian Stewardship 17
       Marriage and the Family 18
       The Lord's Day 19

         Lawful Oaths and Vows.. 19
         Civil Government 19
7.00   God Consummates All Life and History 20
         Death and Resurrection 20
         Judgment and Consummation 21

Preamble to the Constitution.. 22

THE CONSTITUTION
1.0   The Church 24
2.00   Particular Church 24
         Members of a Particular Church 24
         Jurisdiction Over Members of a Particular Church............... 25
         Officers of a Particular Church.. 25
         Organization of a Particular Church..................................... 26
         Government of a Particular Church....................................... 27
         Ministers of the Word and Sacrament 28
         Elders... 30
         Deacons 31
         Election, Ordination, and Installation of Elders and Deacons .. 31
3.00   Judicatories of the Church 34
         Committees and Commissions of Judicatories....................... 35
         References 36
         Of Property 36
4.0   Session.. 37
5.0   Presbytery 39
6.00   The Authority of Presbytery Over Ministers,
         Licentiates, and Candidates 42
         Receiving Candidates 42
         Licensing Candidates 44
         Ordination of Ministers 46
         Recognition of Ordination.. 49
         Jurisdiction over Ministers 50
7.00   Relations Between Ministers, Licentiates,
         or Candidates and Churches 52
         Installation of Pastors and Associate/Assistant Pastors............. 53
8.0   Synod 53
9.0   General Assembly... 55
10.0   Relations Between Churches.. 57
11.0   Amendments.. 59

APPENDICES TO THE CONSTITUTION 61
         Letter of Dismission For Church Members............................ 61
         Certificate of Reception for Church Members 61
         Admission of New Churches.. 62
         Selecting Pastors and Associate/Assistant Pastors 63
         Letter of Dismission for Ministers or Probationers............... 63
         Certificate of Reception for Ministers or Probationers.............. 64

RULES OF DISCIPLINE
1.0   Purpose of Discipline 65
2.0   Authority in Discipline 65
3.00   Discipline of Persons 67
          Cases Without Disciplinary Hearings............................ 67
          Disciplinary Hearings Before Sessions 68
          Specific Procedures for Elders and Deacons............... 73
          Discipline of Ministers 73
          Appeals Regarding the Discipline of Persons 79
4.00   Discipline of Judicatories 82
          General Review and Control 82
          Appeals.. 83
          Dissents and Protests.. 86

DIRECTORY FOR WORSHIP
Preface   81
I.   THE CORPORATE WORSHIP OF GOD 88
       A. The Ordering of Corporate Worship 88
       B. Ordinary Acts of Corporate Worship 90
       C. Basic Resources for Corporate Worship 91
       D. Suggested Orders for Corporate Worship.................... 93
          1. Corporate Worship Including the Lord's Supper.............. 93
          Prelude.. 93
          Opening Sentences 94
          Hymn of Praise 94
          Prayer of Adoration 94
          Confession of Sin and Declaration of Pardon or
             Words of Assurance 94
          Responses of Praise 95
          The Hearing of God's Word.. 95
          Affirmation of Faith or Creed.. 95
          The Prayers of the People... 96
          The Presenting of the Gifts or Offering.......................... 96
          The Celebration of the Lord's Supper............................. 96
          Postlude 98
          Announcements 98
          2. An Order for Corporate Worship Without the
             Lord's Supper.. 99
          3. A Second Order for Corporate Worship Without the
             Lord's Supper.. 99
          4. A Third Order for Corporate Worship Without the
             Lord's Supper.. 100
       E. Orders for Occasional Worship.................................. 100
          Order 1 101
          Order 2.. 101
          Order 3.. 101
          Order 4.. 101
       F.   Leadership of Corporate Worship 102
          General Guidelines.. 102

Symbols and Vestments... 102
    G. The Choir, Musicians and Corporate Worship.......................... 103
    H. The Christian Year and Corporate Worship 103
II. THE SACRAMENTS 104
    A. The Sacrament of Baptism and Corporate Worship 104
    B. Celebrating the Sacrament of Baptism 105
    C. The Sacrament of the Lord's Supper
          and Corporate Worship... 107
          Celebrating the Lord's Supper... 108
III.   LITURGICAL RITES AND OCCASIONAL WORSHIP 109
    A. Public Profession of Faith... 109
          Transfer of Membership or Reaffirmation of Faith 112
    B. Christian Marriage 112
    C. The Christian Funeral 114
    D. Individual and Family Worship 116

RULES OF ORDER
1.0   Moderator 117
2.0   Vice Moderator... 118
3.0   Stated Clerk 119
4.0   Treasurer... 120
5.0   Opening and Closing of Judicatory Meetings 120
6.0   Quorums 121
7.0   Adoption of Program: Orders of the Day 121
8.00 Motions... 122
8.10 Bringing a Motion Before a Judicatory 122
8.20 Considering a Motion 122
8.30 Types of Motions 122
      Main Motion... 122
          Subsidiary Motions 122
          Privileged Motions 123
          Incidental Motions... 124
          Motions that Bring a Question Again Before the Judicatory .. 126
8.40 Miscellaneous Rules Concerning a Motion............................ 127
9.00 Amendments.. 127
          Classification as to Form.. 127
          To Amend by Substitution... 127
          Primary and Secondary Amendments 128
          Improper Amendments 128
10.00 Assignment of the Floor and Debate 128
11.0 Nominations and Elections.. 129
12.0 Voting 129
13.00 Boards, Committees and Commissions................................... 130
14.0 Cases not Provided for in These Rules.................................... 132

INTRODUCTION TO THE 1984 CONFESSION

"For God so loved the world that he gave his only Son, that whoever believes in him should not perish but have eternal life" (John 3:16). This is "the gospel in miniature." It is true testimony to Jesus Christ as Lord and Savior of the world. It has been the testimony of Cumberland Presbyterians from the outset of their origin. It is the statement of the purpose of this confession of faith and its organizing principle.

The purpose of a confession of faith is two-fold: (1) to provide a means whereby those who have been saved, redeemed, and reconciled by God through Jesus Christ in the power of the Holy Spirit understand and affirm their faith; and (2) to bear witness to God's saving activity in such a way that those who have not been saved, redeemed, and reconciled might believe in Jesus Christ as Lord and Savior and experience salvation. To this end a confession of faith is an affirmation of ancient truth in contemporary language. Hence, it should begin with that which is ancient and proceed to speak in language which is natural for those who seek to make witness to God's mighty acts of judgment and redemption in their own time.

The ancient truth which guides this confession of faith is of two sources: (1) the scriptures; and (2) the previous confessions of both Cumberland Presbyterian churches and the previous confessions of the church in its universal expression. All testimony to Jesus Christ must be tested by the scriptures which are the only unfailing and authoritative word for Christian faith, growth, and practice. All testimony to Jesus Christ is made within the context of the church universal and therefore must not be made in a narrow, sectarian manner or spirit.

A confession of faith which is evangelical in purpose and spirit seeks to testify to what God has done and is doing in the world to accomplish the redemption of his children. The scriptures themselves are the best example of how to do this in an organized way. Therefore, the organizing principle of this confession of faith is to tell the story the Bible tells in the way the Bible tells it. We are greatly indebted to the *Confession of Faith* of 1883, the *Confession of Faith* of 1814, and the *Westminster Confession of Faith* out of which the other two arose. We revere these confessions and have drawn from them in writing this confession. The outline of this confession, however, is drawn from the scriptures and is roughly that of the biblical outline found in John 3:16, the topics being as follows: (1) God Speaks to the Human Family; (2) The Human Family Breaks Relationship with God; (3) God Acts Through Jesus Christ to Reconcile the World; (4) God Acts Through The Holy Spirit; (5) God Creates the Church for Mission; (6) Christians Live and Witness in the World, and (7) God Consummates All Life and History.

There is a direct relationship between the church's confession of faith and her life and witness as a people in covenant with God and with each other. The faith of the church orders and shapes the life of the people of God--their mission, their government, their worship, and the orderly conduct of the church's affairs. Believing this, the Cumberland Presbyterian Church and the Cumberland Presbyterian Church in America adopt the following as their testimony to Jesus Christ and as their system of internal government, consisting of: (1) the Confession of Faith; (2) the Constitution; (3) Rules of Discipline; (4) the Directory for Worship, and (5) the Rules of Order.

We send forth this book praying that God will bless with his Spirit this our testimony.

CONFESSION OF FAITH

"For God so loved the world, that he gave his only begotten Son, that whoever believes in him should not perish, but have eternal life." (John 3:16).

1.00 GOD SPEAKS TO THE HUMAN FAMILY

The Living God

1.01 We believe in the only true and living God, Father, Son, and Holy Spirit; who is holy love, eternal, unchangeable in being, wisdom, power, holiness, justice, goodness, and truth.[1]

1.02 The one living God who is Father, Son, and Holy Spirit, the Holy Trinity, speaks through the holy scriptures, the events of nature and history, apostles, prophets, evangelists, pastors, teachers, but uniquely in Jesus Christ, the Word made flesh.[2]

1.03 By word and action God invites persons into a covenant relationship. God promises to be faithful to the covenant and to make all who believe his people. All who respond with trust and commitment to God's invitation find the promise sure and rejoice in being members of God's people, the covenant community.[3]

The Holy Scriptures

1.04 God's words and actions in creation, providence, judgment, and redemption are witnessed to by the covenant community in the scriptures of the Old and New Testaments.[4]

1.05 God inspired persons of the covenant community to write the scriptures. In and through the scriptures God speaks about creation, sin, judgment, salvation, the church and the growth of believers. The scriptures are the infallible rule of faith and practice, the authoritative guide for Christian living.[5]

---

[1]**1.01** Dt. 6:4-5, 32:3-4; 1 Ch. 29:10-12; Ps. 33:4-5, 89:5-18, 99, 102:25-27, 103, 111, 145:8-21; Is. 6:1-3; Mal. 3:6; Jn. 3:16; 1 Co. 8:4-6; 1 Ti. 2:5-6; 1 Jn. 4:7-10; Rev. 1:8, 15:3-4

[2]**1.02** Ex. 3:1-6; Ps. 19:1-6; Mt. 28:18-20; Jn. 1:1-18, 3:16-17; Ac. 7; Ro. 1:18-20; 1 Co. 1:30-31; 2 Co. 13:14; Eph. 4:11-13; Ph. 2:5-11; Col. 1:13-20, 2:8-10; 2 Ti. 3:14-17; He. 1, 2, 5:5-10; 2 P. 1:19-21

[3]**1:03** Gn. 9:8-17; Dt. 7:9; Ps. 36:5, 89:1-5; Jer. 31:31-34; 1 Co. 1:4-9; 2 Co. 3:4-18; He. 8, 9:11-28, 10:19-25

[4]**1.04** Gn. 1-3, 6-8, 11:1-9, 19:1-29, 37, 39-50; Ex. 1:19; 1 K. 17:1-6, 19:4-8; 2 K. 22; Is. 53, 55; Am. 2; Ac. 7; Ro. 4; Gal. 3:6-14; Eph. 1:3-14

[5]**1.05** Gn. 1-3; Ex. 24:3-4; Dt. 31:9-13; Jos. 8:30-35; Jn. 3:16-17, 20:30-31; Ac. 1:16; 1 Co. 2:11-13; Eph. 4:11-16; 2 Ti. 3:14-17; 2 P. 1:19-21, 3:18

1.06   God's word spoken in and through the scriptures should be understood in the light of the birth, life, death, and resurrection of Jesus of Nazareth. The authority of the scriptures is founded on the truth contained in them and the voice of God speaking through them.[6]

1.07   In order to understand God's word spoken in and through the scriptures, persons must have the illumination of God's own Spirit. Moreover, they should study the writings of the Bible in their historical settings, compare scripture with scripture, listen to the witness of the church throughout the centuries, and share insights with others in the covenant community.[7]

*Old Testament

Genesis	I Kings	Ecclesiastes	Obadiah
Exodus	II Kings	Song of Solomon	Jonah
Leviticus	I Chronicles	Isaiah	Micah
Numbers	II Chronicles	Jeremiah	Nahum
Deuteronomy	Ezra	Lamentations	Habakkuk
Joshua	Nehemiah	Ezekiel	Zephaniah
Judges	Esther	Daniel	Haggai
Ruth	Job	Hosea	Zechariah
I Samuel	Psalms	Joel	Malachi
II Samuel	Proverbs	Amos	

*New Testament

Matthew	II Corinthians	I Timothy	II Peter
Mark	Galatians	II Timothy	I John
Luke	Ephesians	Titus	II John
John	Philippians	Philemon	III John
Acts of the Apostles	Colossians	Hebrews	Jude
Romans	I Thessalonians	James	Revelation
I Corinthians	II Thessalonians	I Peter	

God's Will

1.08   God's will for people and all creation is altogether wise and good. Although revealed in the scriptures and in the events of nature and history, God's will is made known supremely in the person of Jesus Christ, who did God's will even to death.[8]

1.09   God's will is sufficiently disclosed for persons to respond to it in worship, love, and service, yet they should hold in reverence and wonder the mystery of divine ways.[9]

---

[6]**1.06** Ps. 119:142, 151-152; Mt. 5:21-48, 17:4-8; Jn. 16:12-15, 17:7-8; He. 1; 1 Jn. 5:9

[7]**1.07** Jn. 14:25-27, 16:12-15; Ac. 15:15-18; I Co. 2:9-13

[8]**1.08** Dt. 18:15-19; Ps. 33:4-5, 34:8; Mt. 26:36-46; Jn. 5:30-47, 10:11-18; Ro. 1:18-23, 2:4; Eph. 1:3-14, 3:1-12; He. 5:7-10

[9]**1.09** Is. 40:12-18, 45:9-11; Ro. 1:18-23, 2:12-16, 11:33-36

Creation

1.10 God is the creator of all that is known and unknown. All creation discloses God's glory, power, wisdom, beauty, goodness, and love.[10]

1.11 Among all forms of life, only human beings are created in God's own image. In the sight of God, male and female are created equal and complementary. To reflect the divine image is to worship, love, and serve God.[11]

1.12 The natural world is God's. Its resources, beauty, and order are given in trust to all peoples, to care for, to conserve, to enjoy, to use for the welfare of all, and thereby to glorify God.[12]

Providence

1.13 God exercises providential care over all creatures, peoples, nations, and things. The manner in which this care is provided is revealed in the scriptures.[13]

1.14 God ordinarily exercises providence through the events of nature and history, using such instruments as persons, laws, and the scriptures, yet remains free to work with them or above them. The whole creation remains open to God's direct activity.[14]

1.15 The purpose of God's providence is that the whole creation be set free from its bondage to sin and death, and be renewed in Jesus Christ.[15]

1.16 God never leaves or forsakes his people. All who trust God find this truth confirmed in awareness of his love, which includes judgment upon sin, and which leads to repentance and to greater dependence upon divine grace. All who do not trust God are, nevertheless, under that same providence, even when they ignore or reject it. It is designed to lead them also to repentance and to trust in divine grace.[16]

1.17 God's providence embraces the whole world, but is especially evident in the creation of the church, the covenant community. Through

---

[10]**1.10** Gn. 1-2; Ex. 20:11; Neh. 9:6; Ps. 19:1-6, 24:1-2, 95:3-7, 104; Jn. 1:1-3; Ac. 14:14-17

[11]**1.11** Gn. 1:26-27, 2:7, 5:1-2; Job 33:4; Ps. 8:3-8, 100:3; Gal. 3:27-28.

[12]**1.12** Gn. 1:26; Ps. 24:1, 50:10-11; Hag. 2:8; 1 Co. 4:7

[13]**1.13** Gn. 4, 6-9, 12-22, 27-33, 35, 37, 39-50; Ex. 1-20, 33; Job 38-41; Ps. 23, 27, 34, 37, 90-91, 105, 107, 121; Is. 25:1-5, 40-45; Mt. 5:45, 6:25-34, 7:7-12, 10:29-31; Ro. 8:28-39; 2 Ti. 1:11-12, 4:14-18; 1 P. 5:6-11

[14]**1.14** Ex. 9:13-16; Jos. 1:5-9; Ps. 135:5-7; Jer. 1:4-10; Mt. 19:26; Lk. 3:8; Ac. 22:12-15, 27:22-25; Ro. 4:18-21

[15]**1.15** Ro. 8:18-23; Eph. 1:9-10; Col. 1:17-20

[16]**1.16** Ps. 94:14-19, 139:7-12; Pr. 15:3; Jer. 23:23-24; Ro. 2:1-16; 2 Co. 12:7-10

patient discipline, God guides this chosen community in her mission of witness and service in the world.[17]

1.18 God's providence is sufficiently displayed to be known and experienced, but, at the same time, it partakes of divine mystery, and is the occasion for wonder, praise, and thanksgiving. Thus even in illness, pain, sorrow, tragedy, social upheaval, or natural disaster, persons may be sure of God's presence and discover his grace to be sufficient.[18]

The Law of God
1.19 God gives the moral law to govern human actions and relations. It is the principle of justice woven into the fabric of the universe and is binding upon all persons.[19]

1.20 The moral law is a gift of God's grace. While it consists of the basic principles of justice revealed in the scriptures and upheld by God, it does not wholly describe the pattern of his actions toward persons. The judgment of God, in which the moral law is upheld, is, at the same time, an expression of redemptive love.[20]

1.21 The moral law is fulfilled in the gospel. Therefore, the behavior of Christians in human relations should reflect the pattern of God's behavior toward them, in which love and justice are intertwined.[21]

1.22 The purpose of the moral law is to create wholeness or health in human life--spiritually, mentally, physically, socially. Therefore, it is the intention of the moral law that the forces of human personality which create integrity of life in all its aspects be used to achieve that wholeness.[22]

2.00 THE HUMAN FAMILY BREAKS RELATIONSHIP WITH GOD

Human Freedom
2.01 God, in creating persons, gives them the capacity and freedom to respond to divine grace in loving obedience. Therefore, whoever will may be saved.[23]

2.02 Because of their God-given nature, persons are responsible for

---

[17]**1.17** Mal. 3:16-18; Mt. 16:18; Ac. 20:28; Ro. 8:28-39; Eph. 5:26-27
[18]**1.18** Job 11:7-10; Is. 40:28-31, 55:8-9; Ro. 11:33-36; 2 Co. 12:7-10
[19]**1.19** Ex. 20-23; Lv. 19:18; Dt. 6:4-9; Ps. 19:7-11; Mic. 6:6-8; Mt. 22:34-40; Ro. 2:12-16, 12:9-10; Gal. 6:7-10; 1 Ti. 1:8-11
[20]**1.20** Ex. 31:18; Ps. 40:8, 103:8-14; Jer. 31:33; Ro. 2:14-16
[21]**1.21** Mt. 5:17-19, 12:1-8; Ro. 3:21-31, 12:9-13, 13:8-10; Gal. 3:21-26; He. 8:8-13
[22]**1.22** Lk. 10:25-28
[23]**2.01** Gn. 1:26-31; Dt. 30:19-20; Is. 55:1-3; Ro. 10:8-13; Rev. 22:17

their choices and actions toward God, each other, and the world.[24]

The Abuse of Freedom

2.03 In rejecting their dependence on God and in willful disobedience, the first human parents disrupted community with God, for which they had been created. They became inclined toward sin in all aspects of their being.[25]

2.04 As did Adam and Eve, all persons rebel against God, lose the right relationship to God, and become slaves to sin and death. This condition becomes the source of all sinful attitudes and actions.[26]

2.05 In willfully sinning all people become guilty before God and are under divine wrath and judgment, unless saved by God's grace through Jesus Christ.[27]

2.06 The alienation of persons from God affects the rest of creation, so that the whole creation stands in need of God's redemption.[28]

3.00 GOD ACTS THROUGH JESUS CHRIST TO RECONCILE THE WORLD

God's Covenant

3.01 God acts to heal the brokenness and alienation caused by sin and to restore the human family to community through the reconciliation effected in Jesus Christ.[29]

3.02 God acts to restore sinful persons to a covenant relationship, the nature of which is that of a family. It is established through God's initiative and the human response of faith.[30]

3.03 God's covenant is a relationship of grace. It appears in various forms and manifestations in the scriptures but always as one of grace. The new covenant in Jesus Christ is its ultimate and supreme expression.[31]

3.04 Jesus Christ, the eternal Word made flesh, is always the essence of the one covenant of grace. Before Christ's coming, it was

[24]**2.02** Gn. 3:1-7; Jos. 24:14-15; Jer. 31:29-30; Ezk. 18:1-4, 26-28; Ro. 1:18-32
[25]**2.03** Gn. 3:1-13, 6:5
[26]**2.04** Gn. 6:5; Ps. 58:3-5, 106:6; Pr. 5:22-23; Is. 59:1-15; Jer. 17:9; Mic. 7:2-4; Jn. 8:34; Ro. 3:9-19, 5:12-14, 6:16, 7:14-20; 2 Ti. 2:24-26; 2 P. 2:17-19
[27]**2.05** Jn. 3:18-19, 36; Ro. 1:18-32, 2:1-9, 3:9-19; Gal. 6:7-8; Eph. 5:5-6
[28]**2.06** Gn. 3:17-18; Ro. 8:18-23; Eph. 1:9-10; Col. 1:19-20
[29]**3.01** Jn. 3:16, 10:7-18, 17:20-23; 2 Co. 5:17-21; Eph. 1:3-10, 2:11-22; Col. 1:15-22
[30]**3.02** Gn. 17:1-7; Ex. 19:3-6, 24:3-8, 34:6-10; Is. 64:8-9; Jer. 31:31-34; Ro. 4:13-25, 8:14-17; Gal. 3:6-9, 26, 4:4-7; He. 11:8-12
[31]**3.03** Gn. 3:15; Ps. 105:7-10, 111:2-9; Mt. 26:26-29; 2 Co. 3:12-18; Gal. 3:13-18, 21-22; He. 8:6-13, 9:11-15, 23-28, 10:1-18

made effective by promises, prophecies, sacrifices, circumcision, the passover lamb, and other signs and ordinances delivered to the people of Israel. These were sufficient through the ministry of the Holy Spirit to instruct persons savingly in the knowledge of God and to lead them to believe God.[32]

3.05 Since Christ's coming, the covenant of grace is made effective chiefly by the preaching of the word and the administration of the sacraments of baptism and the Lord's Supper. In these, together with other acts of worship and acts of love toward the neighbor, the gospel of the covenant of grace is set forth simply and yet in fullness and with spiritual power.[33]

3.06 Children have always been included with their parents in the covenant of grace. Before Christ came, the appropriate sign and seal thereof was circumcision. Since the advent of Christ the sign and seal is baptism.[34]

Christ the Savior

3.07 God's mighty act of reconciling love was accomplished in Jesus Christ, the divine Son who became flesh to be the means by which the sins of the world are forgiven.[35]

3.08 Jesus Christ, being truly human and truly divine, was tempted in every respect as every person is, yet he did not sin. While fully sharing human life, Christ continued to be holy, blameless, undefiled, and thoroughly fitted to be the savior of the world, the only hope of reconciliation between God and sinful persons.[36]

3.09 Jesus Christ willingly suffered sin and death for every person. On the third day after being crucified, Christ was raised from the dead, appeared to many disciples, afterward ascended to God, and makes intercession for all persons.[37]

3.10 Through the Holy Spirit, people are able to acknowledge and repent of their sin, believe in Jesus Christ as Savior, and follow Christ as Lord. Believers experience Christ's presence and guidance, which

---

[32]**3.04** Gn. 3:15; Mic. 5:2; Jn. 8:56-58, 17:24; 1 Co. 10:1-4; Eph. 1:3-10

[33]**3.05** Mt. 28:18-20; 1 Co. 1:17-25, 11:23-26; Col. 2:9-15; 2 Ti. 4:1-2

[34]**3.06** Gn. 17:7-14; Ac. 2:39, 16:15, 33; 1 Co. 1:16; Col. 2:11-12

[35]**3.07** Mt. 1:18-23; Lk. 1:26-38, 67-75, 2:8-13; Jn. 1:14-18, 3:16; Ro. 5:6-11, 8:1-4; 2 Co. 5:17-21; Eph. 1:3-10, 2:4-10; Ph. 2:5-11; Col. 1:15-20; 1 P. 1:3-9, 18-21, 2:21-25; 1 Jn. 4:9-10

[36]**3.08** Mt. 4:1-11; Jn. 1:1-4, 14, 3:13-19, 36, 17:1-5; Ac. 4:12; Ro. 1:1-6; Col. 2:9-10; 1 Ti. 3:16; He. 2:17-18, 4:15, 7:26-28; 1 P. 2:22-25; 1 Jn. 3:5

[37]3.09 Is. 53, 61:1-3; Mt. 26:36-46; Jn. 10:11-18; Ac. 1:3; Ro. 4:23-25, 8:31-34; 1 Co. 15:3-8; He. 2:9, 9:24

helps them to overcome the powers of evil in ways consistent with God's nature and will.[38]

3.11 God's work of reconciliation in Jesus Christ occurred at a particular time and place. Yet its powers and benefits extend to the believer in all ages from the beginning of the world. It is communicated by the Holy Spirit and through such instruments as God is pleased to employ.[39]

4.00 GOD ACTS THROUGH THE HOLY SPIRIT

The Call and Work of the Holy Spirit

4.01 God acted redemptively in Jesus Christ because of the sins of the world and continues with the same intent in the Holy Spirit to call every person to repentance and faith.[40]

4.02 The Holy Spirit works through the scriptures, the sacraments, the corporate worship of the covenant community, the witness of believers in word and deed, and in ways beyond human understanding. The Spirit moves on the hearts of sinners, convincing them of their sins and their need for salvation, and inclining them to repentance and faith toward God.[41]

4.03 The call and work of the Holy Spirit is solely of God's grace and is not a response to human merit. The call precedes all desire, purpose, and intention of the sinner to come to Christ. While it is possible for all to be saved with it, none can be saved without it. Whoever will, therefore, may be saved, but not apart from the illuminating influence of the Holy Spirit.[42]

4.04 Persons may resist and reject this call of the Holy Spirit, but for all who respond with repentance and trustful acceptance of God's love in Christ, there is salvation and life.[43]

Repentance and Confession

4.05 Repentance is that attitude toward God wherein sinners firmly resolve to forsake sin, trust in Christ, and live in grateful obedience to God.[44]

---

[38]**3.10** Jn. 16:8-15; Ac. 13:1-3; Ro. 8:26-27; 1 P. 1:3-9
[39]**3.11** Mk. 15:24-37; Jn. 3:5-8, 6:63; Ro. 8:11; 1 Co. 10:1-4, 12:4-11; 2 Co. 3:4-6; Gal. 3:8; Tit. 3:4-7
[40]**4.01** Jn. 16:7-11; Ac. 7:51; Ro. 3:23-26; 1 Co. 15:3-4; 1 Jn. 2:1-2, 4:9-10; Rev. 22:17
[41]**4.02** Jn. 16:7-11; Ac. 8:29-39, 13:1-3
[42]**4.03** 1 Co. 2:14; Eph. 2:1-10; Tit. 3:4-5; Rev. 22:17
[43]**4.04** Is. 63:10; Jn. 3:14-15, 36, 5:24; Ac. 5:3-4, 7:51; Ro. 10:8-13
[44]**4.05** Mk. 14:72; Lk. 15:18-20, 19:8-10

4.06 Persons do not merit salvation because of repentance or any other human exercise. Yet repentance is necessary to partake of the saving grace and forgiveness of God in Christ.[45]

4.07 In response to God's initiative to restore relationships, persons make honest confession of sin against God, their brothers and sisters, and all of creation, and amend the past so far as is in their power.[46]

Saving Faith

4.08 Saving faith is response to God, prompted by the Holy Spirit, wherein persons rely solely upon God's grace in Jesus Christ for salvation. Such faith includes trust in the truthfulness of God's promises in the scriptures, sorrow for sin, and determination to serve God and neighbor.[47]

4.09 Persons do not merit salvation because of faith, nor is faith a good work. Faith is a gift made possible through God's love and initiative. Yet God requires the response of faith by all who receive salvation and reconciliation.[48]

4.10 When persons repent of sin and in faith embrace God's salvation, they receive forgiveness for their sin and experience acceptance as God's children.[49]

4.11 In the life of faith, believers are tested and suffer many struggles, but the promise of ultimate victory through Christ is assured by God's faithfulness. Both the scriptures and the experiences of the covenant people throughout the centuries witness to this promise.[50]

Justification

4.12 Justification is God's act of loving acceptance of believers whereby persons are reconciled to him by the life, death, and resurrection of Jesus Christ. When they in repentance and faith trust Christ, who is their righteousness, God gives them peace and restores their relationship with him.[51]

4.13 In this relationship God continues to forgive sin. Although

---

[45]**4.06** Ps. 34:18, 51:17; Ezk. 18:21, 30-32; Jl. 2:12-13; Mt. 3:2; Lk. 13:2-5, 17:10; Ac. 3:19, 17:30-31; Eph. 2:8-9; Tit. 3:3-7

[46]**4.07** Ps. 32:5, 51:3-17; Lk. 15:18-20, 19:8-10; Eph. 4:25-31

[47]**4.08** Jn. 6:28-29; Ro. 10:17

[48]**4.09** Jn. 3:14-28, 36; Ac. 16:29-31; Ro. 4:16; Gal. 3:21-22; Eph. 1:13-14; Ph. 3:8-9

[49]**4.10** Jn. 1:11-13, 5:24, 6:28-29, 40; Ro. 1:16-17, 10:8-13; 1 Jn. 5:12

[50]**4.11** Lk. 22:31-32; Jn. 16:33; Ro. 3:3-4, 4:19-21, 8:28-39; 1 Co. 1:4-9, 10:13; 1 Th. 5:23-24; 2 Th. 3:3-5; 2 Ti. 2:11-13; He. 11, 12; 1 Jn. 5:4-5

[51]**4.12** Gn. 15:6; Ps. 32:1-2, 103:8-13, 130:3-8; Lk. 18:9-14; Ac. 13:38-39; Ro. 3:19-31, 4, 5:1-2; 1 Co. 1:30-31; Ph. 3:7-11; 1 P. 1:8-9

believers sometimes disrupt their peace with God through sin and experience separation from God, yet they are assured that it is by God's grace that they are accepted and the relationship is sustained. Only by growth in grace can the believer experience the fullness of relationship with God.[52]

4.14 Those who are reconciled to God through Jesus Christ continue to know a sinful nature. They continue to experience within themselves the conflict between their old selves and their new selves, between good and evil, between their wills and God's will, between life and death.[53]

Regeneration and Adoption

4.15 Regeneration is God's renewal of believers and is solely of God's grace. Those who trust in the Lord Jesus Christ are recreated, or born again, renewed in spirit, and made new persons in Christ.[54]

4.16 Regeneration is necessary because all persons who are separated from Christ are spiritually dead and unable of themselves to love and glorify God.[55]

4.17 Regeneration is accomplished by the Holy Spirit showing sinners the truth of Christ, enabling them to repent and believe God in the light of that truth and to receive the saving grace and forgiveness given in Jesus Christ.[56]

4.18 When empowered by the illuminating influence of the Holy Spirit, believers are able to love and glorify God and to love and serve their neighbors.[57]

4.19 All persons dying in infancy and all who have never had the ability to respond to Christ are regenerated and saved by God's grace.[58]

4.20 Adoption is the action of God to include in the covenant family all who are regenerated and made new persons in Christ. This action assures community with God and one's brothers and sisters in Christ, both now and in the full redemption of the family of God.[59]

---

[52]**4.13** Ps. 32:1-2, 103:8-14, 17-18; Jer. 31:34; Jn. 10:27-30; Ro. 8:1-4; He. 13:5-6; 2 P. 1:3-11
[53]**4.14** Ro. 7:7-25, 8:5-8, 12-13; Gal. 5:16-17; 1 Jn. 1:5-10, 2:15-17
[54]**4.15** Ezk. 36:25-27; Jn. 1:11-13; 2 Co. 5:16-21; Eph. 2:4-10; Tit. 3:3-7; 1 P. 1:23-25
[55]**4.16** Ps. 14:1-3; Mt. 15:18-20; Jn. 3:3-8; Ro. 8:6-7; Gal. 6:15; Eph. 2:1-3
[56]**4.17** Jn. 1:12-13, 3:3-8, 14:25-26, 16:13-15; Tit. 3:4-6
[57]**4.18** 1 Co. 12:3; Gal. 5:22-24; 1 P. 1:22-25, 4:8-11
[58]**4.19** Lk. 18:15-16; Jn. 3:3; Ac. 2:38-39
[59]**4.20** Ro. 8:14-17; Gal. 4:3-7; Eph. 1:5-6

Sanctification and Growth in Grace

4.21 Sanctification is God's setting apart of believers as servants in the world.[60]

4.22 As believers continue to partake of God's covenant of grace, to live in the covenant community, and to serve God in the world, they are able to grow in grace and the knowledge of Jesus Christ as Lord. Believers never achieve sinless perfection in this life, but through the ministry of the Holy Spirit they can be progressively conformed to the image of Jesus Christ, thereby growing in faith, hope, love, and other gifts of the Spirit.[61]

4.23 The struggle with sin continues, for believers are still imperfect in knowledge and the power to do God's will. Their freedom to trust, love, and serve God and neighbors is compromised sometimes by distrust, hate and selfishness. This inner struggle drives them again and again to rely on God's power to conform them to the image of the new person in Jesus Christ.[62]

Preservation of Believers

4.24 The transformation of believers begun in regeneration and justification will be brought to completion. Although believers sin and thereby displease God, the covenant relationship is maintained by God, who will preserve them in eternal life.[63]

4.25 The preservation of believers depends upon the nature of the covenant of grace, the unchangeable love and power of God, the merits, advocacy, and intercession of Jesus Christ, and the presence and ministry of the Holy Spirit who renews God's image in believers.[64]

4.26 As a consequence of temptation and the neglect of the means of grace, believers sin, incur God's displeasure, and deprive themselves of some of the graces and comforts promised to them. But believers will never rest satisfied until they confess their sin and are renewed in their consecration to God.[65]

---

[60]**4.21** Ps. 4:3; Ro. 6:6-14, 20-22; 1 Co. 6:9-11; 2 Co. 6:14-18; 7:1; Eph. 4:17-24, 5:25-27; 1 Th. 5:23-24; 2 Th. 2:13-14; He. 9:13-14; 1 P. 1:1-2

[61]**4.22** Ps. 14:1-3; Ecc. 7:20; Ro. 3:23-24; 2 Co. 3:18, 9:10-11; Eph. 3:14-21; Ph. 2:12-16; Col. 3:5-17; 1 Th. 3:12-13; 2 Ti. 2:20-21; 1 P. 2:2-3; 2 P. 1:3-11

[62]**4.23** Ro. 7:7-25; Gal. 5:16-17; 1 Jn. 2:9-11

[63]**4.24** Ps. 37:27-28; Lam. 3:22-24, 31-33; Jn. 5:24, 10:27-29; Ro. 8:38-39; 2 Co. 4:13-18; Ph. 1:6; 2 Ti. 1:11-12

[64]**4.25** Ps. 23, 34, 91, 121; Jer. 32:40; Jn. 14:16-17; Ro. 5:10; 2 Co. 5:5; 2 Ti. 2:19; He. 7:23-25; 1 Jn. 2:1-2; Jd. 24-25

[65]**4.26** Ps. 32:3-5, 51:1-12; Is. 59:1-2

Christian Assurance

4.27 Believers who seek to know and to do the will of God, and who live in him as he lives in them, may in this life be assured of salvation and thus rejoice in the hope of fully sharing the glory of God.[66]

4.28 This comforting assurance is founded upon the divine promises, the consciousness of peace with God through Christ, and the witness of the Holy Spirit with the believers' spirits that they truly are God's children. Assurance is the promise of the believers' full inheritance.[67]

4.29 This assurance may not immediately accompany initial trust in Christ. It will increase, however, as the believer faithfully participates in the worship, sacraments, ministry, witness, and life of the covenant community, through which God confirms to believers the promise never to leave or forsake them.[68]

5.00 GOD CREATES THE CHURCH FOR MISSION

The Church

5.01 There is one, holy, universal, apostolic church. She is the body of Christ, who is her Head and Lord.[69]

5.02 The church is one because her Head and Lord is one, Jesus Christ. Her oneness under her Lord is manifested in the one ministry of word and sacrament, not in any uniformity of covenantal expression, organization, or system of doctrine.[70]

5.03 The church is holy because she is founded on the finished and continuing work of Christ in setting her apart for God's glory and witness in the world. Her holiness thus rests on God's sanctifying her for her redemptive mission, not upon any personal holiness of her members.[71]

5.04 The church is universal because God's act of salvation in Jesus Christ is universal and cannot be limited to any place or time. Her universal nature rests upon the universal activity of God's Holy Spirit to make Christ's atonement effective for all peoples. It is expressed in the church's commission to make disciples of all nations.[72]

---

[66]**4.27** Ro. 5:1-5; 2 Ti. 1:11-12; 1 Jn. 2:3-6, 5:13

[67]**4.28** Mt. 28:19-20; Ro. 5:1-2, 8:15-17; Eph. 1:13-14; He. 6:17-20, 13:5; 2 P. 1:3-4, 10-11; 1 Jn. 3:2-3, 14-15, 19-24, 4:13

[68]**4.29** Ro. 15:13; He. 6:11-12; 2 P. 1:10-11

[69]**5.01** Mt. 16:18; Jn. 10:16, 17:20-23; Ro. 12:4-5; 1 Co. 10:17, 12:12-27; Eph. 1:22-23, 2:14-22, 3:4-6

[70]**5.02** Mt. 28:18-20; 1 Co. 3:11; Eph. 4:15-16, 5:23; Col. 1:18-20

[71]**5.03** Jn. 17:17-23

[72]**5.04** Gn. 12:1-3; Mt. 8:11, 28:18-20; Jn. 3:16; Gal. 3:28; He. 2:9; Rev. 7:9-10

5.05 The church is apostolic because God calls her into being through the proclamation of the gospel first entrusted to the apostles. The church thus is built on the apostolic message which is faithfully proclaimed by messengers who follow in the footsteps of the apostles.[73]

5.06 The church, as the covenant community of believers who are redeemed, includes all people in all ages, past, present, and future, who respond in faith to God's covenant of grace, and all who are unable to respond, for reasons known to God, but who are saved by his grace.[74]

5.07 The church in the world consists of all who respond in faith to God's saving grace and who enter into formal covenant with God and each other. The children of believers are included in this covenant community and are under the special care and instruction of the church and their parents or guardians.[75]

5.08 Because the church in the world consists of persons who are imperfect in knowledge and in the power to do God's will, she waits with eager longing for the full redemption of the family of God. Until that time God wills that all believers worship and witness through the church in the world and promises to guide her life and growth through the Holy Spirit.[76]

5.09 The church in the world never exists for herself alone, but to glorify God and work for reconciliation through Christ. Christ claims the church and gives her the word and sacraments in order to bring God's grace and judgment to persons.[77]

Christian Communion

5.10 All who are united to Christ by faith are also united to one another in love. In this communion they are to share the grace of Christ with one another, to bear one another's burdens, and to reach out to all other persons.[78]

5.11 The communion of believers has special meaning for members of the same organized body. Beyond this particular community believers have special relationship with other organized bodies who

---

[73]**5.05** Mt. 28:18-20; Jn. 20:21-23; Ac. 10:42-43; Ro. 10:14-18; 1 Co. 1:21-25, 15:1-11; 2 Co. 5:18-21; 1 P. 1:10-12

[74]**5.06** Gn. 12:1-3, 17:1-7; Mt. 8:11; Gal. 3:26-29; He. 12:18-24; Rev. 7:9-10

[75]**5.07** Gn. 17:7; Dt. 6:4-9; Is. 40:11; Mt. 19:13-15; Ac. 2:39; 1 Co. 7:13-14; Eph. 6:1-4

[76]**5.08** Mt. 5:14-16, 13:24-30, 47-50, 28:18-20; Ac. 1:6-8; 1 Co. 12:4-11

[77]**5.09** Is. 49:6; Mt. 5:14-16, 28:19-20; Jn. 15:1-11; 2 Co. 5:14-21

[78]**5.10** Ro. 12:9-21; Gal. 5:13-14, 6:1-2; Ph. 2:1-7; 1 Th. 3:12-13, 5:11-15; He. 13:1-3; 1 P. 4:8-11

embrace similar creeds, historical heritage, and forms of the covenant community.[79]

Christian Worship

5.12 Christian worship is the affirmation of God's living presence and the celebration of God's mighty acts. It is central to the life of the church and is the appropriate response of all believers to the lordship and sovereignty of God.[80]

5.13 In worship God claims persons in Christ and offers assurance of love, forgiveness, guidance, and redemption. Believers respond to God with praise, confession, thanksgiving, love, and commitment to service.[81]

5.14 Christian worship includes proclaiming the gospel of Jesus Christ, celebrating the sacraments, reading and hearing the scriptures, praying, singing, and committing life and resources to God. This common worship of the church validates and sustains such other worship as the church finds meaningful for celebrating the living presence of God.[82]

5.15 God is to be worshiped both corporately and privately. Corporate worship is practiced in the gathered congregation, in small groups within the church, and in larger gatherings of believers. Private worship, through meditation, prayer, and study of the scriptures, is practiced in various settings, especially in the home by individuals and by the family.[83]

Sacraments

5.16 Sacraments are signs and testimonies of God's covenant of grace. Circumcision and passover are the sacraments of the Old Testament; baptism and the Lord's Supper are the sacraments of the New Testament. They are given by God and through his presence, word, and will are made effective.[84]

5.17 Jesus Christ ordained the sacraments of baptism and the Lord's Supper for the church. They are administered by and through the church as part of her common worship, being entrusted to properly ordained ministers under the authority of a judicatory of the church.[85]

[79]**5.11** Ps. 133; Ac. 2:42-47
[80]**5.12** Ps. 29:1-2, 95:1-7, 96:1-9, 145:4-7; Mt. 4:10; Jn. 4:22-24
[81]**5.13** Ps. 89:1-2, 100, 150; Eph. 5:18-20; He. 13:15; 1 P. 2:9-10
[82]**5.14** Ac. 2:44-47, 10:34-48, 20:7-11; 1 Ti. 2:1-10; He. 10:19-25
[83]**5.15** Jos. 24:15; Mt. 6:6-13; 1 Co. 14:26-33; Eph. 5:18-20
[84]**5.16** Gn. 17:9-14; Ex. 12:21-27; Mt. 26:26-29, 28:19-20; Ro. 4:11
[85]**5.17** Mt. 28:19-20; Mk. 14:22-25; 1 Co. 10:16-17, 11:23-26

Baptism

5.18 Baptism symbolizes the baptism of the Holy Spirit and is the external sign of the covenant which marks membership in the community of faith. In this sacrament the church witnesses to God's initiative to claim persons in Christ, forgive their sins, grant them grace, shape and order their lives through the work of the Holy Spirit, and set them apart for service.[86]

5.19 The sacrament of baptism is administered to infants, one or both of whose parents or guardians affirm faith in Jesus Christ and assume the responsibilities of the covenant, and to all persons who affirm personal faith in Jesus Christ and have not received the sacrament.[87]

5.20 Water is the element to be used in this sacrament. The person receiving the sacrament is to be baptized in the name of the Father and of the Son and of the Holy Spirit.[88]

5.21 In administering the sacrament the pouring or sprinkling of water on the person by the minister fittingly symbolizes the baptism of the Holy Spirit; however, the validity of the sacrament is not dependent upon its mode of administration.[89]

5.22 It is the privilege and duty of all believers to seek baptism for themselves and their children, and to accept its benefits. However, baptism is neither an indispensable condition of salvation nor effective apart from life in Christ and the church.[90]

The Lord's Supper

5.23 The Lord's Supper was instituted by Jesus Christ on the night of his betrayal. It is a means by which the church remembers and shows forth Christ's passion and death on the cross. The sacrament is also a perpetual means given to the church to celebrate and experience the continuing presence of the risen Lord and her expectation of the Lord's return.[91]

5.24 The elements used in this sacrament are bread and the fruit of the vine, which represent the body and blood of Christ. The elements themselves are never to be worshiped, for they are never anything other than bread and the fruit of the vine. However, because the sacrament represents the Savior's passion and death, it should not be received

---

[86]**5.18** Mt. 3:11-12; Ac. 2:38-41, 10:44-48

[87]**5.19** Ac. 16:14-15, 32-33; 1 Co. 1:16

[88]**5.20** Mt. 28:19; Ac. 8:36-39, 10:47-48

[89]**5.21** Ac. 2:33, 10:45; Tit. 3:4-7

[90]**5.22** Ac. 8:36-38, 16:15, 33; 1 Co. 1:16

[91]**5.23** Mt. 26:26-29; 1 Co. 10:16-17, 11:23-26

without due self-examination, reverence, humility, and grateful awareness of Christ's presence.[92]

5.25 This sacrament is a means of spiritual nourishment and growth, an act of grateful obedience to Christ, and a commitment to the work and service of Christ's church for all who celebrate it.[93]

5.26 All persons who are part of the covenant community and are committed to the Christian life are invited and encouraged to receive this sacrament.[94]

5.27 Each congregation should celebrate this sacrament regularly. Every Christian should receive it frequently.[95]

The Church in Mission

5.28 The church, being nurtured and sustained by worship, by proclamation and study of the word, and by the celebration of the sacraments, is commissioned to witness to all persons who have not received Christ as Lord and Savior.[96]

5.29 Growth is natural to the church's life. The church is called into being and exists to reach out to those who have not experienced God's grace in Christ, and to nourish them with all the means of grace.[97]

5.30 In carrying out the apostolic commission, the covenant community has encountered and continues to encounter people who belong to religions which do not acknowledge Jesus Christ as Lord. While respecting persons who adhere to other religions, Christians are responsible to share with them the good news of salvation through Jesus Christ.[98]

5.31 The covenant community is responsible to give witness to the mighty acts of God in the life, death, and resurrection of Jesus Christ. Where and when this witness is lacking, God is not without a witness. Therefore, it does not belong to the covenant community to judge where and in what manner God acts savingly through Jesus Christ.[99]

Church Government

5.32 Jesus Christ as Lord and Head of the church has entrusted

---

[92]**5.24** Mt. 26:26-29; 1 Co. 5:7-8, 11:27-34

[93]**5.25** Ac. 2:42, 46-47; 1 Co. 11:23-26

[94]**5.26** Mt. 26:26-28; 1 Co. 11:28-32

[95]**5.27** 1 Co. 14:40

[96]**5.28** Is. 43:10, 49:6; Mt. 28:19-20; Lk. 24:45-49; Ac. 1:6-8, 5:30-32, 10:39-42, 22:14-15; 1 P. 2:9

[97]**5.29** Mt. 13:33, 28:19-20; Jn. 21:15-17; Ac. 2:41, 4:4, 6:7, 9:31; Eph. 4:10-16

[98]**5.30** Ac. 8:26-40, 10:34-48, 13:16-48, 14:1-3, 14-17, 17:22-31

[99]**5.31** Mt. 28:19-20; Ac. 10:34-35; 14:16-17, 17:22-31; Ro. 2:12-16

the government of the church to officers who make those decisions that will guide the life and ministry of the covenant community.[100]

5.33 These officers have the responsibility to serve the church, to examine and receive members into the communion of the church, to care for and nurture them in the faith, and to discipline with love and justice those who offend the gospel and the laws of the church.[101]

Church Judicatories

5.34 The Cumberland Presbyterian Church and Cumberland Presbyterian Church in America are governed by certain representative bodies: session, presbytery, synod, and General Assembly. Each of these church bodies in its special areas of responsibility has legislative, judicial, and executive authority, yet all are to be conducted in recognition of their interdependence and Christian mission.[102]

5.35 It is the responsibility of these representative bodies, consistent with the church's constitution, to determine matters of faith, practice, and government, propose forms of worship and witness, exercise discipline, and resolve appeals properly brought before them.[103]

6.00 CHRISTIANS LIVE AND WITNESS IN THE WORLD

Christian Freedom

6.01 Through Jesus Christ, God frees persons from the shackles, oppression, and shame of sin and sinful forces, from the guilt and penal consequences of sin, and enables them to have free access to God. This freedom, rooted in love, not fear, enables persons to become who God intends them to be, to bear witness to their Lord, and to serve God and neighbors in the vocations of their common life.[104]

6.02 While God alone is Lord of the conscience and in matters of faith and worship God frees believers from the opinions and commandments of others that are contrary to his word, this does not preclude their need for the instruction and discipline of the church.[105]

6.03 Believers who, under the pretext of Christian freedom practice sin, thereby violate the nature and purpose of Christian freedom.

[100]**5.32** Ac. 1:21-26, 6:1-6, 14:23, 15:6-22; Ph. 1:1; 2 Ti. 3:1-13, 5:17-22

[101]**5.33** Mt. 18:15-20; Ac. 20:28-31; 1 Co. 5:1-5; 1 Th. 5:12-14; 1 Ti. 5:17-22; Tit. 1:5-9; 1 P. 5:1-5

[102]**5.34** Ac. 14:23, 15:6-29, 16:4; 1 Ti. 4:13-16, 5:17-22; Tit. 1:5-9

[103]**5.35** Mt. 18:15-17; Ac. 15:6-29

[104]**6.01** Jn. 8:31-36; Ac. 5:29-32, 40-42; Ro. 6:12-23, 7:24-25, 8:1-17, 14:4; 1 Co. 8-9, 10:23-33; Gal. 3:1-14, 5; Eph. 2:18, 3:11-12; 1 Jn. 4:18

[105]**6.02** 1 Co. 8, 12:12-27

Believers are free to love and serve the Lord rather than evil.[106]

6.04 Believers who, under the pretext of Christian freedom, defy the proper exercise of just and lawful authority, either civil or ecclesiastical, are subject to the discipline of the church.[107]

6.05 Christians owe ultimate allegiance to Jesus Christ as Lord, and must never yield that ultimate allegiance to any government or nation, and should in Christian conscience oppose any form of injustice.[108]

Good Works

6.06 Believers are saved by grace through faith which produces the desire to do the good works for which God creates persons in Christ Jesus.[109]

6.07 Good works are done in thankful response to the gift of God's grace. God graciously accepts the works of believers despite their many weaknesses and imperfect motives.[110]

6.08 Good works are the result of and not the means of salvation.[111]

6.09 Good works encompass not only those deeds of service and mercy exemplified by Christ, but also those ethical and moral choices that reflect Christian values and principles in all of life's relationships.[112]

Christian Stewardship

6.10 Christian stewardship acknowledges that all of life and creation is a trust from God, to be used for God's glory and service. It includes the conservation and responsible use of natural resources as well as the creative use of human skills and energies. These gifts of God are to be shared with all, especially with the poor.[113]

6.11 The motive for Christian stewardship is gratitude for God's abundant love and mercy, accompanied by the desire to share all of God's good gifts with others.[114]

6.12 God gives to the human family a variety of gifts, including gifts to each person for which each person has responsibility. God

---

[106]**6.03** 1 Co. 8; 1 P. 2:16

[107]**6.04** Mt. 18:17; Ro. 13:1-2; 1 Co. 5; Tit. 3:1; He. 13:17; 1 P. 2:13-16

[108]**6.05** Mt. 6:24; Ac. 4:5-31, 5:27-32; Rev. 19:10

[109]**6.06** Ps. 116:12-14; Ro. 11:5-6; Eph. 2:4-10; Tit. 3:4-7

[110]**6.07** Mk. 5:18-20; Lk. 7:47-50, 19:8-9

[111]**6.08** Lk. 6:43-45; Gal. 5:22-25

[112]**6.09** Is. 58:6-7; Mt. 25:31-46; Lk. 10:29-37; He. 6:9-12, 13:1-5; Ja. 1:19-27, 2:8-26; 1 P. 2:11-25

[113]**6.10** Gn. 1:26-31; Ps. 8:3-8, 24:1, 50:10-12; Ac. 4:32-37, 20:33-35; 1 Co. 4:7; Gal. 2:9-10; Ja. 1:17, 2:1-7

[114]**6.11** Lk. 21:1-4; Ac. 4:34-37, 9:36-41; 2 Co. 8:1-15

desires that each person engage in the mutual sharing of these gifts so that all may be enriched.[115]

6.13 Proportionate and regular giving of all that God entrusts to the human family is an act of devotion and a means of grace. Giving to and through the church is the privilege of every believer. Tithing as a scriptural guide for giving, is an adventure of faith and a rich and rewarding practice. The tither not only experiences the grace of God but even the grace of sharing.[116]

6.14 All believers are responsible to God and to the covenant community for their stewardship.[117]

Marriage and the Family

6.15 God created the family as the primary community in which persons experience love, companionship, support, protection, discipline, encouragement, and other blessings. It is the normal relationship into which children are born.[118]

6.16 The church recognizes and ministers to people living in a variety of family patterns, including those persons who by choice or circumstances are single. It seeks to embrace each person and all groups of persons within the family life of the covenant community.[119]

6.17 Marriage is between a man and a woman for the mutual benefit of each, their children, and society. While marriage is subject to the appropriate civil law, it is primarily a covenant relationship under God. As such, it symbolizes the relationship of Jesus Christ and the church, and is that human relationship in which love and trust are best known.[120]

6.18 As a covenant relationship under God, marriage is a lifetime commitment, and should not be taken lightly.[121]

6.19 Because marriage is primarily a covenant relationship under God, between a man and a woman, it is morally wrong and unlawful for any person to have more than one living marriage partner.[122]

6.20 When human weakness and sin threaten a marriage relationship, the covenant community has responsibility to uphold the sanctity of

---

[115]**6.12** Mt. 25:14-30; 1 Co. 12:4-26, 13, 16:1-2; Eph. 4:1-16; 1 P. 4:10-11

[116]**6.13** Gn. 28:22; Dt. 14-22; Mal. 3:8-11; Mt. 23:23; 1 Co. 16:1-2

[117]**6.14** Mt. 12:36-37; Lk. 12:16-21, 47-48; Ro. 14:10-12; 1 Co. 4:1-2; 2 Co. 5:9-10

[118]**6.15** Gn. 1:26-31, 2:8-24; Pr. 31:10-31; S. Sol. 8:7; Mt. 19:3-12; 1 Co. 13; Eph. 6:1-4; Col. 3:18-21

[119]**6.16** Ac. 4:34-35; 1 Co. 7, 12:14-26; 1 Jn. 2:12-14

[120]**6.17** Gn. 2:18-24; Is. 54:5-6; Eph. 5:21-33; Rev. 19:7-8, 21:2-3,9

[121]**6.18** Gn. 2:21-24; Ro. 7:2

[122]**6.19** Gn. 2:24; 1 Co. 7:2

marriage and to help partners strengthen their relationship. If a marriage is dissolved by divorce, the covenant community is responsible to minister to the victims, including any children of the marriage, and to counsel divorced persons who are considering remarriage.[123]

6.21 The church has responsibility to help persons prepare for marriage, for parental responsibilities, and for family life under the lordship of Jesus Christ.[124]

6.22 The church has responsibility to minister to the needs of persons in every crisis, including physical and emotional illness, economic distress, natural disasters, accidents due to carelessness, and death.[125]

The Lord's Day

6.23 The Creator has given one day in seven for special reflection on God's nature and deeds. From the beginning of the world to the resurrection of Christ the seventh day of the week, known as the sabbath, was the Lord's Day. Subsequent to Christ's resurrection, Christians celebrate the first day of the week as the Lords' Day.[126]

6.24 Appropriate activities on the Lord's Day include worship, study, doing good works, and other activities leading to renewal. The proper observance of the Lord's Day enriches the quality of life for all other days.[127]

Lawful Oaths and Vows

6.25 Christians should bind themselves by oath or pledge only to those good and just promises they are reasonably able to perform.[128]

6.26 A vow is similar to an oath and should be made with care, performed with faithfulness, and honored with integrity. Persons should vow to do only that which is consistent with the scriptures.[129]

Civil Government

6.27 The purpose of civil government is to enable God's creation to live under the principles of justice and order. As it faithfully upholds the welfare of God's creation, civil government lies within the purpose

---

[123]**6.20** Mt. 5:31-32; 1 Co. 12:12-27

[124]**6.21** Eph. 5:21-33, 6:1-4

[125]**6.22** Ac. 2:44-45, 4:32-37, 6:1-3; Ro. 12:4-21; 1 Co. 12:14-27; Gal. 6:1-2; Col. 3:12-14; 1 Th. 5:14-15

[126]**6.23** Gn. 2:2-3; Ex. 20:8-11, 23:12; Jn. 20:19; Ac. 20:7

[127]**6.24** Is. 58:13-14; Mt. 12:1-14; Jn. 7:23-24; 1 Co. 16:1-2

[128]**6.25** Lv. 19:12; Ps. 116:12-14; Ecc. 5:2

[129]**6.26** Nu. 30:2; Dt. 23:21-23; Ecc. 5:4-5; Mt. 5:33-37

of God and functions as a useful instrument to enable people to live in harmony and peace.[130]

6.28   It is the duty of people to participate in civil government in such ways as are open to them, especially in exercising the right to vote. It is the duty of Christians to enter civil offices for which they are qualified and for the purpose of working for justice, peace, and the common welfare.[131]

6.29   Civil government and persons elected to civil office may not assume control over or administration of the church in matters of faith or practice. Yet their duty is to protect the religious freedom of all persons and to guard the right of religious bodies to assemble without interference.[132]

6.30   The covenant community, governed by the Lord Christ, opposes, resists, and seeks to change all circumstances of oppression--political, economic, cultural, racial--by which persons are denied the essential dignity God intends for them in the work of creation.[133]

6.31   The covenant community affirms the lordship of Christ who sought out the poor, the oppressed, the sick, and the helpless. In her corporate life and through her individual members, the church is an advocate for all victims of violence and all those whom the law or society treats as less than persons for whom Christ died. Such advocacy involves not only opposition to all unjust laws and forms of injustice but even more support for those attitudes and actions which embody the way of Christ, which is to overcome evil with good.[134]

6.32   God gives the message and ministry of reconciliation to the church. The church, corporately and through her individual members, seeks to promote reconciliation, love, and justice among all persons, classes, races, and nations.[135]

7.00 GOD CONSUMMATES ALL LIFE AND HISTORY

Death and Resurrection

7.01   Death is both a spiritual and physical reality.   Therefore the church has the privilege and duty to proclaim that in Jesus Christ,

---

[130]**6.27** 2 S. 23:3-4; 2 Ch. 19:5-7; Ps. 72:1-4, 82:1-4; Ro. 13:1-7; 1 Ti. 2:1-2; 1 P. 2:13-17
[131]**6.28** Mt. 17:27, 22:15-21; Ro. 13:1-7; 1 Ti. 2:1-3; Tit. 3:1; 1 P. 2:13-17
[132]**6.29** 2 Ch. 26:16-18
[133]**6.30** Dt. 15:7-11; Ps. 41:1-3, 82:3-4; Pr. 21:13, 29:4, 14
[134]**6.31** Mt. 9:35-38, 14:14, 15:32-39; Ro. 12:19-21
[135]**6.32** Mt. 28:18-20; 2 Co. 5:18-20

God acts to redeem persons from bondage to death both in spirit and body.[136]

7.02 Those who have been regenerated in Christ live with joyful and confident expectation that after death their redemption will be complete in the resurrection of the body.[137]

7.03 As in regeneration the whole person is resurrected to new life in Christ, so in the resurrection of the dead the whole person is raised to live in and enjoy the presence of God forever.[138]

7.04 Believers are assured of having passed from the death of sin into life with God. They confidently await full redemption without fear of judgment. Thanks be to God who gives this victory through the Lord Jesus Christ![139]

Judgment and Consummation

7.05 The judgment of God is both present and future. Persons experience God's judgment in many forms, including broken relationships with God and others, the guilt and consequences of their own actions, and the sense of anxiety that comes from lack of confidence in God's faithfulness and the purpose of life.[140]

7.06 God's judgment is experienced in history in the freedom of persons and nations to choose to engage in such evils as war, civil strife, slavery, oppression, destruction of natural resources, and political and economic exploitation. God abhors all such acts which cause needless suffering and death.[141]

7.07 God's judgment transcends this life, ever standing against all human attempts to deny dependence on God and to live without repentance, faith, and love. Those who reject God's salvation in Jesus Christ remain alienated from God and in hopeless bondage to sin and death, which is hell.[142]

7.08 In the consummation of history, at the coming of Jesus Christ, the kingdoms of the world shall become the kingdom of the Lord and of the Christ, and he shall reign forever and ever.[143]

---

[136]**7.01** Gn. 2:17, 3:19; Job 14:1-2, 10-12, 30:23; Ps. 103:15-16; Jn. 5:24, 11:25-26; Ac. 4:1-2, 17:17-18, 30-31, 24:14-15; Ro. 5:12; 1 Co. 15:12-57; Eph. 2:1-8; 2 Ti. 1:8-10; He. 2:14-15; Ja. 1:15; 1 P. 1:3-5; 1 Jn. 3:14; Rev. 1:17-18

[137]**7.02** Ro. 8:11; 1 Co. 15:12-57; 2 Co. 5:1-10; Ph. 3:20-21; 1 Th. 4:13-18; 1 P. 1:3-9; 1 Jn. 3:1-2

[138]**7.03** 1 Th. 4:13-19, 5:9-10

[139]**7.04** Jn. 3:14-18, 36; 1 Co. 15:51-57; 2 Co. 5:1-5; 1 Jn. 3:1-2, 5:12

[140]**7.05** Ecc. 12:13-14; Mt. 25:31-46; Jn. 3:16-21, 5:25-29; Ac. 17:29-31; Ro. 14:7-12; 2 Co. 5:9-10; He. 9:27-28; 2 P. 2:4-10, 3:5-10; Rev. 20:11-15, 21:8

[141]**7.06** Mal. 3:5; Ro. 2:1-3; Gal. 6:7-8

[142]**7.07** Lk. 16:19-31; Jn. 3:18-21, 36; He. 9:27-28; Rev. 20:11-15

[143]**7.08** 1 Co. 15:22-28; Rev. 11:15-18, 12:10-12

Preamble to the Constitution

The form of church government is the structure through which the activities of government are carried out. The purpose of church government is to aid the church in performing its mission. This Constitution in drawn according to the Presbyterian form, and its purpose is that the Cumberland Presbyterian Church/ Cumberland Presbyterian Church in America may be governed in such a manner that the church will perform its mission.

Cumberland Presbyterian congregations are found around the world. While the mission of the church is the same everywhere, the forms and structures of the Constitution and Rules of Discipline do not always fit seamlessly with the cultures, traditions, and legal systems of some countries. In countries other than the United States the provisions of the Constitution and Rules of Discipline should be applied so far as possible, but the Constitution and Rules of Discipline are, at heart, documents which exist to promote spiritual objectives. If there are instances in which the letter of the Constitution and/or Rules of Discipline cannot be applied without compromising the mission of the church and the spiritual objectives identified in the Confession of Faith, it is the spirit of the law, rather than the letter, which must prevail.

Although no detailed form of church government is laid down in scripture, the connectional nature of the church is clearly affirmed. The Presbyterian form embodies the connectional nature of the church in a manner compatible with scripture. In the Old Testament, during the period of the monarchy in Israel, church government was mixed with and sometimes controlled by civil government. After the destruction of the national state of Israel and during the Babylonian captivity, the synagogue emerged as the organizational form of the covenant community. Its government was a prototype of the Presbyterian form.

Jesus and his apostles worshiped and taught in the synagogue. Paul's missionary activity in a city usually was begun in the synagogue. As the followers of Jesus came to be known as Christians, and the movement gradually separated from Judaism, its government developed along the lines of the synagogue.

The form of government inherited from the synagogue was a representative system in which a group of persons, called elders, acted for the people in matters relating to the life of the synagogue. The Greek word that is translated elder is *presbuteros* (presbyter). An assembly of elders is *presbuterian* (presbytery). Hence the name Presbyterian.

Although the first leaders among the followers of Jesus were called apostles, this term seems to have been restricted to those who had seen the risen Christ and who had been commissioned personally by him. With the death of the apostles, the term elder, already in use, became the accepted title that designated the highest church leaders.

The New Testament recognized two kinds of elders, those who are ministers of word and sacrament, and those lay persons who assist them. All elders share in the government of the church. The term bishop (*episkopos*), used less frequently in the New Testament seems to have been a synonym for elder.

In addition to the office of elder, the New Testament refers to a group of lay leaders called deacons. Derived from the Greek word *diakonos*, which means servant, this title designated those who had a special responsibility in the care of the poor and others in need.

In the government of the church elders function as a representative body. The levels of government recognized in the New Testament are that of the particular church (session), the region (presbytery), and the whole church (synod or assembly).

THE CONSTITUTION

1.0 THE CHURCH

1.1   By the covenant with Abraham and his descendants according
to faith, God has established the church in the world through his Son
Jesus Christ. This household of faith, the universal church, consists
of all those persons in every nation and every age who confess Jesus
Christ as Lord and Savior and who respond to his call to discipleship.

1.2   As the universal church cannot assemble at one time and
place, it exists in the world as particular churches gathered together for
worship, study, witness, and service.

2.00 PARTICULAR CHURCH

2.01   A particular church is a congregation of professing Christians,
together with their baptized children, who have entered into a covenant
with each other to meet together regularly to worship God and study the
word of God, to join together in a common witness to the gospel, and to
engage in the good works to which Christians are called; and who have
adopted a certain form of government.

2.10 Members of a Particular Church

2.11   The members of a particular church who are entitled to all
rights and responsibilities of the church, consist of those persons who
have confessed Jesus Christ as Lord and Savior, entered into the church
covenant, and received the sacrament of baptism.

2.12   The session has responsibility to examine and instruct in
church membership those who unite with a particular church.

2.13   Children of believers are, through the covenant, entitled
to the sacrament of baptism and thereby become members of the
household of faith. Such children are to receive pastoral oversight,
instruction, and the care of the church, with a view that they repent of
sin, personally confess Jesus Christ as Lord and Savior, and assume the
full responsibilities of church membership.

2.14   Baptized persons who have not confessed Jesus Christ as Lord
and Savior, even though they are adults, should continue to receive
the watchful care and instruction of the church in the hope that they
personally will own their faith.

2.15   Unbaptized persons who have not confessed Jesus Christ as
Lord and Savior are within the pastoral concern of the church in the

hope that they may be led to repentance and to faith in Jesus Christ as Savior.

2.20 Jurisdiction Over Members of a Particular Church

2.21 A church member is under the jurisdiction of the session of the particular church to which he or she belongs.

2.22 A letter of dismission from a particular church shall not be given to the church member but directed to another particular church of the Cumberland Presbyterian Church/Cumberland Presbyterian Church in America or that of another ecclesiastical body.

2.23 The session of a particular church may receive a person who has confessed faith in Jesus Christ and been a member of another church by transfer of letter. If reasonable attempts to obtain a letter fail, the particular church may receive the person on reaffirmation of faith and notify the person's former church of its action. The same procedure may be used for churches whose policy is not to grant letters of dismission.

2.24 A member dismissed by letter from a church of the Cumberland Presbyterian Church/ Cumberland Presbyterian Church in America shall be under the jurisdiction of the session granting the letter until notification of reception by the session of the church to which the letter is granted or until creditable knowledge is had by the session granting the letter of reception into some church.

(Forms for Letters of Dismission and Certificates of Reception, see Constitution, Appendices 1 and 2, respectively.)

2.25 When a church member moves beyond the bounds of the particular church to which he or she belongs and neglects to request a letter of dismission or fails to retain the status of an active member, his or her name shall be entered on the church's roll of inactive members. Record of the transaction shall be made in the minutes of the session and the member shall be informed of the action by the session.

2.26 When a person, for any reason, desires to cease to be a member of the church, the name of the person shall be removed from the membership roll providing no charges are pending against him or her or he or she is under no disciplinary action. The name shall not be removed from the membership roll, however, until an effort is made to counsel with the person.

2.30 Officers of a Particular Church

2.31 The officers of a particular church are the minister in charge, who is ordained to proclaim the gospel and administer the sacraments;

the elders who are members of the session, who are elected and ordained as the representatives and leaders of the people; and the deacons who are members of the diaconate, who are elected and ordained to care for the poor and others in need.

2.40 Organization of a Particular Church

2.41 A particular church can be organized only by the authority of the presbytery. In considering the formation of a new church, the presbytery shall be involved in the planning. Upon approval of presbytery for the organization of the church any minister who is a member of presbytery may preside at the organization and perform all the duties required, except where a commission for that purpose shall have been appointed by presbytery. The new church shall not be located within three miles of an existing church of the Cumberland Presbyterian Church/Cumberland Presbyterian Church in America without the approval of presbytery.

2.42 The steps in organizing a particular church are as follows:

a. Letters of transfer, or testimonials of current church membership, shall be presented by those who are members of a church. Others may be admitted to membership on reaffirmation of faith or on confession of faith in Christ, the church covenant, baptism (or confirmation of baptism) and examination as necessary.

b. These persons shall then be required to enter into covenant, by answering affirmatively the following question: *Do you, in reliance upon God for strength, solemnly promise and covenant with God and each other that you will walk together as an organized church according to the government of the Cumberland Presbyterian Church/Cumberland Presbyterian Church in America; that you will support the gospel as God has prospered you; that you will maintain this church, not only with your gifts, but also with your support of its work by your efforts and prayers; that you will seek in its fellowship to glorify the name and further the cause of our Lord Jesus Christ; and that you will work to maintain the purity and harmony of the whole body?*

c. After this, the presiding minister shall say: *I now declare that you are constituted a church according to the word of God and the government of the Cumberland Presbyterian Church/ Cumberland Presbyterian Church in America. In the name of the Father, and of the Son, and of the Holy Spirit. Amen.*

d. The members of the church shall proceed, with the presiding minister in charge, to determine the number of elders to be elected to constitute the session and the type of tenure to which they shall be elected and to elect elders. The ordination and installation of the elders may follow immediately or at a later date. At the option of the members, deacons may be elected, ordained, and installed at this time, at a subsequent congregational meeting, or not at all.

e. The presiding minister, or the commission appointed by the presbytery, shall be responsible for reporting on the organizational service, including a recommendation that the newly organized church be enrolled as a constituent member, at the next regular meeting of the presbytery. The report should include the date of organization, location, names of those acting on behalf of presbytery to organize the congregation, number of charter members and the list of officers elected.

(Forms for Admission of New Churches, see Constitution, Appendix 3).

2.50 Government of a Particular Church

2.51 Responsibility for the government of a particular church belongs to the session, which is composed of the minister in charge and the elders elected by the congregation and installed as members of the session. The session thus constituted is responsible to lead the members in all those ministries which belong to the church:

a. Public worship, including praying, singing of praises, reading the scriptures, presenting tithes and offerings, preaching the word, and celebrating the sacraments:

b. Christian education, including study of the scriptures for Christian growth;

c. Activities of fellowship appropriate to the family of God;

d. Personal witness to unbelievers and to those out of fellowship with the church;

e. Visitation of the sick;

f. Pastoral care of families, especially disturbed and broken families;

g. Stewardship of time, talents, and money, and the care and use of the properties of the church;

h. Exercise of discipline.

i. Participation in the ministry of the church beyond the bounds of the local congregation; and in such other ministries as appear needful. Leading the people in these ministries may be done by appointing them to serve with elders on various committees representing different areas of ministry; and by directing them as individuals in the life of the church.

2.52 In a particular church which is without a pastor, the elders who constitute the session are themselves responsible, within the limits of their offices, to lead the people in all the ministries that belong to the church.

2.53 A congregational meeting of the members of a particular church shall be convened for the following purposes:
  a. To determine the type of tenure of office for elders and deacons;
  b. To nominate, elect, or accept the resignation of elders and deacons;
  c. To establish a quorum of the session or diaconate as less than a majority of the members;
  d. To recall an elder or deacon whose service is no longer acceptable to the church;
  e. Where state law or presbytery requires it, to authorize the sale and purchase of church property.

2.54 A congregational meeting may be convened also to provide an opportunity for communication between the session and the congregation on other matters, but without the procedure of voting.

2.55 A congregational meeting of the members of a church shall be held when authorized by the session, or at the request of 15% of the total membership of the church, or when directed by the presbytery. Notice of the meeting shall be given either by written notice to the entire membership at least one week before the meeting or by announcement on the three Sundays before the meeting, or by some other method which the session judges to be adequate notice. The minister in charge, or in a church without a pastor, a minister designated by presbytery, shall serve as moderator of the congregational meeting. The clerk of the session shall record the minutes of the meeting, which shall be approved at the next meeting of the session and made a part of its records. A quorum for a congregational meeting shall consist of those members present at the appointed time and place.

2.60 Ministers of the Word and Sacrament

2.61 The office of minister of word and sacrament is unique in the life of the church as to responsibility and usefulness. God calls persons and sets them apart for this ministry. The persons who fill this office should be sound in the faith, exemplary in conduct, and competent to perform the duties of the ministry. Persons who become ministers of the word and sacrament are due such respect as belongs to their office, but are not by virtue of their office more holy or righteous than other Christians. They share in the same vocation that belongs to all Christians to be witnesses to the gospel in word and deed. They differ from other Christians only with regard to the office to which they are called, which is their station in life.

2.62 The person who fills the office of the ministry has in the scriptures different titles, expressive of various duties:

pastor--who has oversight of the people and feeds them with spiritual food and administers the sacraments as signs of God's grace;

minister--who serves Christ in all those ministries to people which belong to the church;

elder or presbyter--who shares in the leadership and government of the church;

evangelist--who bears the glad tidings of salvation through Jesus Christ, appealing to sinners to be reconciled to God;

prophet--who urges people and nations to heed the word of God, warning of the consequences of disobedience;

priest--who intercedes with God through prayer on behalf of others;

preacher--who publicly proclaims the gospel of Christ;

teacher--who explains the scriptures emphasizing the lessons essential to Christian growth.

These titles do not confer privilege in the church nor designate different grades of office but indicate the scope of responsibilities that belong to the office of ministry.

2.63 A minister who is called to be the pastor of a particular church is responsible to:

a. lead the people in public worship;
b. pray for and with them as their mouth to God;
c. read the scriptures to the people and proclaim to them the word of God;
d. administer the sacraments;
e. bless the people from God;
f. teach the scriptures to the children, youth, and adults;
g. visit the people, especially the poor, the sick, the dying, and those with other critical needs;
h. counsel with persons in their preparation for marriage;
i. share in the personal witness of the church to unbelievers and those out of fellowship with the church;
j. counsel with people, in light of the scriptures, about their personal needs and problems;
k. counsel with disturbed and broken families;
l. and with the elders who comprise the session, lead and govern the

church in all its ministries.

2.64   While the type of ministry most basic to the life of the church is that of a pastor, God has given different gifts to ministers of the word and sacrament and the church recognizes various types of ministry. Presbytery may authorize ministers to exercise their gifts not only as pastors of particular churches but as teachers of religion in various kinds of schools, editors of religious publications, chaplains to the military forces and to various types of institutions, missionaries, evangelists, counselors, administrators of church programs and institutions, directors of Christian education in particular churches, and as leaders in other fields of service directly related to the church. Presbytery shall authorize persons to perform such types of ministry through a service of worship in which the minister is commissioned to practice his or her ministry in one of these ways. In every type of ministry, the minister should seek appropriate ways to perform the duties as pastor, minister, presbyter, evangelist, prophet, priest, preacher, and teacher.

2.70 Elders

2.71   Elders are the immediate representatives of the people, elected by them to share with ministers in the government and leadership of the church. The elders who comprise the session share with the minister in charge in the pastoral oversight of the particular church.

2.72   In caring for and leading the congregation which they serve, elders shall be particularly attentive to persons who have not confessed Jesus Christ as Lord and Savior, those who are spiritually weak, and those who need to be instructed in the faith. They shall visit the people in their homes, praying with and for them, especially for the sick, those who mourn, and others in need. They should encourage the people by word and example to share in the worship, study, witness and service of the church through a faithful stewardship of their time, talents, and money. They should inform the pastor of any concerns that need his or her attention.

2.73   Persons who fill the office of elder may be male or female, young or old. Elders share in the same vocation that belongs to all Christians to be witnesses to the gospel, but the vocation of this office places an additional responsibility of leadership upon them. They should exemplify the gospel by their good character, sound faith, wisdom, maturity of judgment, discretion, conversation, knowledge of the doctrine and government of the church, and competency to perform the duties of the office.

2.74   Persons who accept the responsibilities of the office of elder should engage in such study and preparation as are appropriate to the office, and during their tenure on the session shall continue to study in order better to perform their duties.

2.80 Deacons

2.81 Deacons are elected by the people and ordained to lead the church in its care of the poor and others in need, administering the funds provided by the church for these purposes. This ministry is given to the church by Jesus Christ, who came to serve rather than to be served. Through the care of the poor and others in need, the church gives witness to the compassionate love of God shown in Jesus Christ. The deacons shall lead and coordinate activities of persons, committees, and groups in ministering to the poor, the elderly, the sick, orphans, refugees, prisoners, and others in distress. Because the work of the deacons pertains to the whole church, the deacons shall make periodic reports to the session.

2.82 In churches desiring to do so, the session may grant to the diaconate power to formulate budgets and assume other financial responsibilities.

2.83 Persons who fill the office of deacon may be male or female, young or old. Deacons shall have sound judgment, good character, compassion for those in need, availability to people, and a deep abiding faith in Jesus Christ, whose example in ministry they follow. Persons who accept the responsibility of the office of deacon shall engage in such study and preparation as are appropriate to the office, and during their tenure on the diaconate shall continue to study in order better to perform their duties.

2.84 The desirability for a diaconate is to be determined by each particular church. In churches where it is impractical to create a diaconate, the duties of the office of deacon shall be assumed by the elders. If a diaconate is created, no person shall serve simultaneously on the session and the diaconate.

2.90 Election, Ordination, and Installation of Elders and Deacons

2.91 In the organization of a particular church, the elders and deacons shall be nominated and elected by the members participating in the organization. In all other cases, it is proper and advisable for the session to nominate, or to cause to be chosen a committee of the congregation at large to nominate, to the congregation at a meeting called to elect elders and deacons, persons to fill these offices. Other nominations may be made by other members of the church, with the approval of the persons being nominated. The vote may be taken on the nominees at the meeting in which they are presented or at a subsequent congregational meeting. Unless by acclamation, the vote shall be by secret ballot, with a majority of votes cast necessary for election. When there are more nominees than positions to be filled, those receiving the highest number of votes are elected.

2.92   When persons have been elected to the office of elder or deacon, the session shall appoint a day for their ordination and/or installation. Persons previously ordained shall be installed only. On the appointed day, with the congregation assembled for worship, the session shall convene for the service of ordination. The minister in charge shall state in a concise manner the nature and responsibilities of the office of elder/ deacon and describe the Christian conduct to be maintained. Having done this, the minister in charge shall propose to the candidate(s) the following questions to be answered in the affirmative:

I.   Do you believe the scriptures of the Old and New Testaments to be the inspired word of God, the authority for faith and practice?

II. Do you sincerely receive and adopt the *Confession of Faith* of the Cumberland Presbyterian Church/Cumberland Presbyterian Church in America as containing the essential doctrines taught in the holy scriptures?

III. Do you approve of and promise to uphold the government of the Cumberland Presbyterian Church/Cumberland Presbyterian Church in America?

IV. Do you promise to promote the peace, unity, and purity of the church?

V.   (*To elders*) In participating as an elder in the judicatories of the church, do you promise to share in a responsible way in the decisions that are made, to abide by those decisions, and to promote the welfare of the church?

VI. Do you accept the office of elder/deacon in this church, and promise faithfully to discharge all the duties thereof as God may enable you?

The installation of previously ordained elders/deacons shall consist in asking Question VI.

These questions being answered in the affirmative, the minister shall put the following question to the congregation:

Do you, the members of the church, acknowledge and receive these elders/deacons, and do you promise to give them such encouragement, support, and respect as belongs to the office?

This question having been answered in the affirmative, the candidates shall kneel. The members of the session shall gather around them. As the minister offers an appropriate prayer, the elders shall, by the laying on of hands, set the candidates apart to the office of elder/deacon.

Then, with all standing, the minister shall say:

I now declare that you have been regularly elected, ordained, and installed elders/deacons in this church, agreeable to the word of God and according to the government of the Cumberland Presbyterian Church/Cumberland Presbyterian Church in America. In the name of the Father, and of the Son, and of the Holy Spirit. Amen.

Members of the session shall take the newly installed officers by the hand and say:

We give you the hand of Christian fellowship to take part in this office with us.

The minister shall then deliver to the newly installed officers and the congregation an appropriate charge.

2.93 Persons may be elected to the session/diaconate for an indefinite period or for definite terms on a rotation basis. In the organization of a church, one type of tenure shall be adopted for the session/diaconate. In an existing church, a change in the type of tenure shall be by actions to dissolve the session/diaconate, install the new type of tenure, and elect members to the session/diaconate according to the new type of tenure. Such actions shall be taken by the congregation in a congregational meeting. If a particular church chooses to elect elders/deacons for a definite term on a rotation basis, the term of office shall be for not less than three years, except when classes are established in the institution of the rotation plan or in cases of unexpired terms.

2.94 If members of the session/diaconate fail to attend half of the stated meetings in a given year without excuse, or if for other non-disciplinary reasons they become unacceptable to the church in the performance of their duties, the session may convene a congregational meeting to consider their removal from office by recall. Before such action is taken, however, opportunity shall be given to the persons involved to address the congregation.

2.95 When elders/deacons move to such a distance that they are unable to fulfill the duties of the office or to participate regularly in the worship, study, witness, and service of the congregation, the session may recommend to the congregation that their tenure of office be terminated. If an elder/deacon is dismissed from the church by letter, the tenure of office is terminated automatically, and this fact shall be recorded by the session in its minutes.

2.96 When elders/deacons are admitted by letter to membership in another church, they may become members of the session/diaconate in that church only by election and installation.

3.00 JUDICATORIES OF THE CHURCH

3.01 Since the government of the church should have order and be effective, it is necessary that it possess clear and reasonable form. The legislative, administrative, and judicial bodies, sometimes referred to as judicatories, are, in regular gradation, session, presbytery, synod, and the General Assembly.

3.02 The connectional nature of the church is expressed in the following governmental structure. The session exercises pastoral oversight and jurisdiction over a particular church; the presbytery over ordained ministers, sessions, and churches within a prescribed area; the synod over presbyteries, ministers, sessions, and churches within a prescribed area; and the General Assembly over synods, presbyteries, ministers, sessions, and churches.

3.03 The authority of each level of church government is limited by the stated provisions of the Constitution. Although each judicatory exercises exclusive original jurisdiction over all the matters specifically belonging to it, the lower judicatories are subject to the review and appellate authority of the next higher judicatory.

3.04 Every properly constituted unit of church government on any level has the right to resolve questions of doctrine and discipline properly and seriously proposed, and in general to maintain truth and righteousness, and to condemn erroneous opinions and practices which would injure the peace, purity and progress of the church.

3.05 All meetings of judicatories shall be opened and closed with prayer.

3.06 Called meetings of presbytery, synod, and the General Assembly shall be composed of the same representatives, or their alternates, who constituted the preceding stated meeting, unless the judicatory elects someone else as its representative. An elder whose tenure of office on the session has expired is not eligible to serve as a representative to a called meeting of a judicatory. A called meeting of a judicatory may be rescinded when a majority of those signing the request for the called meeting communicate in writing with the Moderator, or in the Moderator's absence or illness the Stated Clerk, their desire to rescind the call. This request must be made in writing at least five days before the called meeting.

3.07 Other ministers [who are not members of the body],who are present in a meeting of presbytery or synod may or may not be seated by the action of the body as advisory members, which if granted gives them the privilege to speak to any matter before the body. Persons so seated shall be introduced to the presbytery or the synod by the moderator.

Comment: Except for persons who are designated as advisory members by right, persons whose presence would assist the judicatory in the accomplishment of its work can always be seated as advisory members and granted permission to speak to the judicatory by a majority vote or common consent.

3.071 The following persons shall be seated by a judicatory as advisory members with full privilege of speaking to any issue before the judicatory, but no vote:
  a. In sessions, assistant and associate pastors approved and installed by the presbytery.
  b. In middle judicatories, elected officers of the judicatory, (for example, stated clerk, engrossing clerk, and treasurer), and official representatives from the judicatory's standing committees or boards.

3.072 The following persons may, with the approval of the judicatory, be seated as advisory members of the judicatory upon their introduction by the moderator:
  a. In middle judicatories, visiting ordained Cumberland Presbyterian ministers and elders.
  b. Elected youth advisory delegates.
  c. Representatives from higher judicatories
  d. Visiting ministers or leaders from other denominations with which the judicatory is in partnership.
  e. Any other person whose presence would, in the judgment of the judicatory, serve the mission and ministry of the judicatory.

3.08 Minutes and all other official records of sessions, presbyteries, synods, and general assemblies are the property in perpetuity of said judicatories or their legal successors. When congregations, presbyteries, or synods are dissolved, their records are held for them by the next highest judicatory within whose bounds they were before dissolution. All minutes and other official records of existing and dissolved sessions, presbyteries, and synods, or copies thereof, are to be deposited for safe keeping in the Historical Foundation of the Cumberland Presbyterian

Church and the Cumberland Presbyterian Church in America. It is the responsibility of the clerk of each judicatory to make recommendation to the judicatory for the permanent safe keeping of that judicatory's records.

3.10 Committees and Commissions of Judicatories

3.11 Each judicatory may, in order to exercise its proper oversight and authority, form standing and/or *ad hoc* committees as it deems appropriate and elect or appoint persons to such committees. Such committees shall examine, consider, and recommend to the judicatory various measures for promoting the work of the judicatory.

3.12 Each judicatory may appoint commissions which are authorized to deliberate upon and conclude the business submitted to them, subject to the review of the judicatory. Full records of a commission's proceedings must be submitted to the appointing judicatory, and, if approved, may be entered in the minutes of that judicatory. A majority of a commission shall constitute a quorum. Commissions may be appointed for purposes such as the following:

a. Ordination of ministers, in which case the commission must contain a quorum of the presbytery, including two ministers;
b. Installation of pastors and associate/assistant pastors;
c. Organization of new churches;
d. Taking testimony in or conducting disciplinary hearings;
e. Visitation of congregations experiencing disorder;
f. Hearing appeals;
g. Investigation of any specified problem in the church.

3.20 References

3.21 Each judicatory except the highest may seek the formal advice of the judicatory immediately higher through reference. A reference is a representation, in writing, to the judicatory immediately higher, of a matter not yet decided by the lower judicatory. A judicatory which makes reference must have all the testimony and documents duly prepared and in readiness for the action or counsel of the higher judicatory. A reference shall be made by vote of the judicatory.

3.22 A reference may be appropriate in cases which involve new, difficult, or delicate matters about which the lower judicatory may be undecided or of divided opinion.

3.23 References may be made for the purpose of counsel, preparatory to a decision by the lower judicatory, in which case the reference suspends decision of the matter in the lower judicatory; or references may submit the entire case to the judgment of the higher judicatory for ultimate decision by it.

3.24 The judicatory receiving a reference is not required to give counsel or make a decision but may remit the matter to the judicatory by which it was referred.

3.25 References may in some cases be proper; yet it is generally for the good of the church that every judicatory exercise its own judgment.

3.30 Of Property

This section is declaratory of principles to which the Cumberland Presbyterian Church/ Cumberland Presbyterian Church in America and their antecedent church bodies have adhered from the inception of the presbyterian form of church government.

3.31 The provisions of church government as set forth in the Constitution, Rules of Discipline, and Rules of Order prescribing the manner in which decisions are made, reviewed, and corrected within this church are applicable to all matters pertaining to property.

3.32a The Cumberland Presbyterian Church is a connectional church and all lower judicatories of the church to-wit: synod, presbytery, and the particular churches are parts of that body and therefore all property held by or for a particular church, a presbytery, a synod, the General Assembly, or the Cumberland Presbyterian Church, whether legal title is lodged in a corporation, a trustee or trustees, or an unincorporated association, and whether the property is used in programs of the particular church or of a more inclusive judicatory or retained for the production of income, and whether or not the deed to the property so states, is held in trust nevertheless for the use and benefit of the Cumberland Presbyterian Church.

3.32b The Cumberland Presbyterian Church in America is a connectional church and all lower judicatories of the church to-wit: synod, presbytery, and the particular churches are parts of that body and therefore all property held by or for a particular church, a presbytery, a synod, the General Assembly, or the Cumberland Presbyterian Church in America, whether legal title is lodged in a corporation, a trustee or trustees, or an unincorporated association, and whether the property is used in programs of the particular church or of a more inclusive judicatory or retained for the production of income, and whether or not the deed to the property so states, is held in trust nevertheless for the use and benefit of the Cumberland Presbyterian Church in America.

3.33 Whenever property of, or held for, a particular church ceases to be used by the church, as a particular church of the Cumberland Presbyterian Church/Cumberland Presbyterian Church in America in accordance with this Constitution, such property shall be held, used, applied, transferred or sold as provided by the presbytery in which that particular church is located.

3.34 Whenever a particular church is formally dissolved by the presbytery, or has become extinct by reason of dispersal of its members, the abandonment of its work, or other cause, such property as it may have shall be held, used, and applied for such uses, purposes, and trusts as the presbytery in which said particular church is located may direct, limit, and appoint, or such property may be sold or disposed of as the presbytery may direct, in conformity with this Constitution.

3.35 A particular church shall not sell, convey, lease, pledge, mortgage, or encumber its real property used for purposes of worship, nurture, or ministry without the written permission of the presbytery in which the particular church is located, transmitted through the session of the particular church. In granting its permission, the presbytery does not become a party to the church's agreement, nor a guarantor of any indebtedness.

4.0 SESSION

4.1 The session of a particular church consists of the minister in charge and elders elected by the congregation. There must be a minimum of two elders, but the actual number shall be determined by the congregation in accordance with such rules as it may establish.

4.2 In a church which has no pastor, or in the absence of the minister in charge or of the moderator appointed by presbytery, the session may meet and transact any business.

4.3 The session may be convened when two or more of its members so request. The minister in charge may convene the session at any time during or immediately following a regular service of worship and at other times by giving proper notice to session members.

4.4 A majority of the session constitutes a quorum unless the congregation has set a quorum otherwise; but any two elders, in conjunction with the minister may receive members and grant letters of dismission.

4.5 The session is charged with pastoral oversight of the particular church and has the responsibility to:

a. Call a pastor (also an associate/assistant pastor) subject to the approval of presbytery;
   (Form for issuing a call to a pastor or associate/assistant pastor, see Constitution, Appendix 4.)
b. Receive members into the church;

c. Resolve questions of doctrine and discipline in the congregation;
d. Admonish or suspend members found guilty in a disciplinary hearing, subject to appeal to presbytery;
e. Urge upon parents the importance of presenting their children for baptism;
f. Grant letters of dismission, which when given for parents shall always include the names of their baptized children;
g. Ordain and install elders and deacons when elected and require these officers to devote themselves to their responsibilities;
h. Examine the proceedings and supervise the work of the deacons;
i. Establish and give oversight to church schools, Bible classes, fellowship and other organizations within the church, with special attention being given to nurture of the children;
j. Encourage the stewardship of church members, order and supervise collections for Godly purposes, and in general, oversee the finances of the church;
k. Assemble the congregation and provide for worship when there is no minister;
l. Initiate and coordinate the best measures for promoting and extending the work of the church;
m. Elect representatives to the higher church judicatories, and require on their return a report of their diligence and the decisions of the judicatory;
n. Observe and carry out the injunctions of the higher judicatories.

4.6 The session may designate two elders, either of whom, when authorized by the presbytery, may administer the sacrament of the Lord's Supper to the congregation. (This applies only to the Cumberland Presbyterian Church.)

4.7 The members of the session, excluding the minister, are the trustees of the church. They shall hold title to the property of the church and shall execute all transactions required by civil law. If it seems desirable the session may elect a smaller number of persons to serve as trustees. In this instance the trustees may act only as specifically authorized by the session. The tenure of office of such trustees may be for an indefinite period or for definite terms on a rotation basis.

4.8 Each session shall keep an accurate record of its proceedings which must be submitted to presbytery, at least annually, for review. Each session shall also keep a record of congregational meetings, of marriages, of baptisms, of additions, and of the death and dismission of church members.

5.0 PRESBYTERY

5.1   A presbytery consists of the ordained ministers and the elders elected to represent the session of the churches within a prescribed area. Presbyteries may be organized on the basis of geographical boundaries or, where the prosperity and enlargement of the church would justify it, on the basis of a common language other than English. Ordinarily, a non-geographical presbytery may overlap the bounds of geographical presbyteries.

5.2   A minister of the Cumberland Presbyterian Church/ Cumberland Presbyterian Church in America who has become a minister of a larger parish composed of denominational units, at least one of which is associated with another church; a minister of a union church; a minister for a limited time of a congregation of another church; or a professor of religion in a college or seminary of another church, may with the approval of the presbytery, accept for a period of such service, ministerial membership in another denomination or denominations. Such additional membership, in whatever manner conferred, shall not alter said minister's status as a minister of the Cumberland Presbyterian Church/ Cumberland Presbyterian Church in America or terminate or modify any of the solemn obligations which the minister assumed by giving affirmative answer to the questions put by the presbytery at the time of ordination.

5.3   A minister of another church with whom the General Assembly has a reciprocal agreement whose ecclesiastical relations have been certified by that church, who has become the minister of a congregation or of a larger parish composed of denominational units, at least one of which is associated with this church, a minister of a union church or a minister of a church outside of the United States with whom the General Assembly has a reciprocal agreement who is serving in a ministerial capacity in this church, including employment as a professor in a college or seminary of this church, may be enrolled for the period of such service as a member of the presbytery and have temporarily the rights and privileges of such membership.

5.4   The session of every particular church shall be entitled to one or more representatives in the presbytery. In a particular church having an active membership of 1 to 300, the session shall be entitled to send one elder as its representative to presbytery; in a particular church having an active membership of 301 to 600, the session shall be entitled to send two elders as representatives to presbytery, and the basis for representation shall continue in the above proportion. Elder representatives may be required to give proper evidence of their election by the session they represent.

5.5   The presbytery, having met at the time and place appointed, may proceed to business provided a quorum of four persons (ministers and session representatives) are present, including at least one minister and one elder.

5.6   The presbytery is charged with pastoral oversight and has the responsibility to:

a. Receive, examine, dismiss, and license candidates and ordain them to the ministry.

b. Receive, dismiss, install, remove, and discipline ministers; *(Forms for Dismission and Reception of Ministers, see Constitution Appendices 5 and 6, respectively.)*

c. Approve ministers to serve as pastors and in other types of ministry;

d. Require ministers to devote themselves diligently to their sacred calling and censure and otherwise discipline the delinquent;

e. Review the records of the sessions, discipline sessions for whatever they may have done contrary to order, and take effectual care that they observe the government of the church;

f. Examine and decide appeals, protests, and referrals brought before it in an orderly manner;

g. Establish the pastoral relation and dissolve it at the request of one or both of the parties, or where the interests of religion imperatively demand it;

h. See that the injunctions of the higher judicatories are obeyed;

i. Condemn erroneous opinions which hinder the peace or purity of the church, and resolve questions of doctrine and discipline properly and seriously proposed;

j. Visit particular churches, inquire into their condition, and redress the evils that may have arisen in them;

k. Settle differences regarding church property and its use;

l. Approve the location of new churches and the relocation of existing churches;

m. Approve proposals and plans of churches considering building or rebuilding church facilities or additions;

n. Unite or divide such churches as are in a chronic state of crisis or inaction, unite or divide other churches with the consent of a majority of the members thereof, and, for cause, dissolve a church and attach its members to another congregation;

o. Form and receive new churches and concert measures for the enlargement of the church within its bounds;

p. Take special oversight of churches which do not have the services of a minister, appointing a minister to moderate the session; and, if necessary, authorize two elders designated by the session to administer the Lord's Supper to the congregation, provided that the elders shall be instructed by the committee on the ministry in the meaning of the sacrament and how it should be administered; the elders shall serve under the authority of an ordained Cumberland Presbyterian minister selected by the presbytery, and each grant of authority shall be for one year;

q. Formulate budgets and assign shares to the churches of the presbytery;

r. Institute and oversee the agencies necessary in the work of the presbytery;

s. In general, order whatever pertains to the welfare of the churches under its care;

t. Elect representatives to the higher judicatories;

u. Propose to the synod or to the General Assembly such measures as may be for the good of the church or of society in general.

5.7   The presbytery shall keep full and accurate records of its proceedings and submit them to the synod for review at its stated meeting. It shall report regularly to synod and to the General Assembly its roll, including all candidates, licentiates, ministers, session clerks, and churches. In addition, it shall report on licensures and ordinations; on reception, dismission, or death of ministers; on the union, division, and formation of churches, and on such statistical and other information as may be required to describe the state of religion in its midst.

5.8   The presbytery shall meet as often as once a year on its own adjournment, and when an emergency shall require a meeting sooner than the time to which it stands adjourned, the moderator, or in case of the moderator's absence, death, or inability to act, the stated clerk shall with written concurrence or at the written request of two minister members and two session members of different churches, call a special meeting. The call shall give notice, specifying the particular business of the intended meeting, to every minister and session of every particular church on its roll, at least ten days prior to the proposed time of meeting. Nothing shall be transacted at such called meeting other than the particular business for which the presbytery was convened.

5.9   If, for any cause, the presbytery shall fail to meet according to its adjournment, it shall be the duty of the moderator, or, in case of the moderator's absence, death, or inability to act, the stated clerk, or in case of the stated clerk's absence, death, or inability to act, persons constituting the equivalent of a quorum, to call a meeting as early as practicable, at such a place as may be designated, for transaction of the regular business. For this purpose notice shall be given, as before prescribed, not less than ten days prior to the proposed time for meeting.

6.00 THE AUTHORITY OF PRESBYTERY OVER MINISTERS, LICENTIATES, AND CANDIDATES

6.10 Receiving Candidates

6.11 Every presbytery shall have a committee on the ministry or one which performs the same functions, one of which shall be to direct and nurture persons in preparation for the ministry.

6.12 To be received as a candidate for the ministry, a person must be a member in good standing of a particular church in the receiving presbytery. Persons desiring to become candidates for the ministry shall confer with the committee on the ministry prior to presenting themselves to presbytery.

6.13 Those who seek to be licensed and ordained to the ministry shall undergo a period of training and preparation in order that the office may be committed only to qualified persons. In order to form a correct judgment of the qualifications of those seeking admission to the office of the ministry, presbyteries shall receive and, following satisfactory preparation, license candidates who shall then be designated "licentiates." Such persons shall be required to give further satisfactory evidence of their qualifications for the ministry before receiving ordination.

6.14 The committee on the ministry shall examine candidates respecting personal religious experience, motives leading to the seeking of the office of the ministry and the internal call to it, and plans for education. Such prior examination by the committee shall not preclude examination by the presbytery at the time of reception. A written statement concerning the candidate from the session of his or her church shall also be heard at the time of reception, along with written or verbal testimonials from others who may desire to express themselves on behalf of the candidate.

6.15 The reception of candidates for the ministry shall be at a duly constituted meeting of presbytery. Following the examination of the candidate and the various testimonials that may be given, a member of the committee on the ministry or a person appointed for that purpose shall address the candidate as follows:

*The Presbytery of_____of the
Cumberland Presbyterian Church/Cumberland Presbyterian Church
in America, having heard the testimonials on your behalf and having
sustained your examination thus far, now requires you to make answer
to the following questions:*

I.   As far as you know your heart, do you believe yourself to be called by God to the office of the Christian ministry.

II. Do you promise, in reliance upon the grace of God, to maintain a Christian character and conduct, and to be diligent and faithful in making full preparation for the ministry?

III. Do you promise to work with the presbytery through its committee on the ministry in matters that pertain to your preparation for the ministry?

IV. Do you now desire to be received by this presbytery as a candidate for the ministry in the Cumberland Presbyterian Church/ Cumberland Presbyterian Church in America?

Following formal reception by the presbytery, the person presiding shall offer an appropriate prayer. Following the prayer, with the congregation standing, the person presiding shall address the candidate as follows:

In the name of the Lord Jesus Christ, the great Head of the church, I do now declare by the authority of this presbytery that you are acknowledged and received as a candidate for licensure and ordination in the Cumberland Presbyterian Church/Cumberland Presbyterian Church in America and I now direct that your name be entered on the roll of the presbytery as a candidate for the ministry.

The person presiding shall then extend to the candidate the hand of Christian fellowship, saying:

The Lord bless you and keep you; the Lord make his face to shine upon you and be gracious unto you; the Lord lift up the light of his countenance upon you and give you peace; through Jesus Christ our Lord. Amen.

Proper record of the reception shall be made in the minutes of presbytery.

6.16 Presbytery may remove the name of a candidate from its roll at any time, but not without indicating the reasons therefor. A candidate may at any time request that his or her name be removed from the roll, which may be done at the next stated meeting of presbytery.

6.17 Upon being received by presbytery, a probationer who is a member of the session of his or her church may remain in that position by mutual agreement of the Committee on the Ministry and the Church

Session. The probationer, however, may not be elected to represent the church at any of the higher judicatories.

6.18 A candidate may be granted a letter of dismission to another presbytery, but the presbytery is not bound to receive the letter. The receiving presbytery may give the candidate the regular examination above stated. A candidate transferring to another presbytery must unite with a particular church in the presbytery to which he or she transfers.

6.200 Licensing Candidates

6.201 Licensure is a judgment by presbytery that a candidate for the ministry has exhibited certain qualities and abilities suitable to the office of ministry and has achieved a certain level of preparation for the ministry. This judgment shall be based on a prior examination of the candidate by the committee on the ministry as to his or her personal spiritual growth; understanding of the nature of the church and its ministry; knowledge of the scriptures, theology, and church history; oral and written use of the native language; and knowledge of any other subjects integral to this level of preparation. Vocational and psychological testing administered by professionals is advisable as part of the process of examination. The report of the committee on the ministry of its examination shall not preclude examination by the presbytery.

6.202 No candidate shall be licensed who has not completed an undergraduate degree from a college or university approved by the presbytery. Exceptions may be made only of persons possessing suitable gifts and abilities for a fruitful ministry, but who, because of reasons considered valid in the judgment of the presbytery, cannot complete an undergraduate degree. In such cases the candidate shall not be licensed until he or she has completed satisfactorily, under the direction of the committee on the ministry, a three-year program of alternate studies approved by the General Assembly.

6.203 The licensing of candidates shall be done at a duly constituted meeting of the presbytery or by a commission of the presbytery meeting at a previously designated time and place. The commission shall consist of a quorum of presbytery, but must include two ordained ministers. After a brief statement as to the meaning and significance of licensure, the person presiding shall propose the following questions to the candidate:

I.   Do you believe the scriptures of the Old and New Testaments to be the inspired word of God, the authority for faith and practice?

II. Do you sincerely receive and adopt the Confession of Faith of the Cumberland Presbyterian Church/Cumberland Presbyterian Church in America as containing the essential doctrines taught in the holy scriptures?

III. Do you promise to promote the peace, unity, and purity of the church?

IV. Do you promise continued cooperation with the presbytery through its committee on the ministry as you continue preparation for ordination, and as you perform those functions of ministry which pertain to a licentiate, as set forth in the Constitution?

The questions being answered in the affirmative, the person presiding shall offer a prayer appropriate to the occasion. Following the prayer, with the congregation standing, the person presiding shall address the candidate as follows:

In the name of the Lord Jesus Christ, the great Head of the church, and by the authority which he has given to the church for its edification, the presbytery now licenses you to preach the gospel and perform other functions of ministry as set forth in the Constitution. To this end may the blessing of God rest upon you and the Spirit of Christ fill your heart. Amen.

Proper record of the licensure shall be made in the minutes of presbytery.

6.204 A licentiate may preach the gospel within the bounds of presbytery or elsewhere with the approval of all presbyteries involved.

6.205 A licentiate may, with the approval of the committee on the ministry of the presbytery and of the presbytery, serve as a stated supply of one or more particular churches of the presbytery.

6.206 A licentiate may serve as stated supply in congregations of other presbyteries, but only with the approval of the committees on the ministry of both or all presbyteries involved and the approval of the presbyteries. In such cases there should be a close working relationship between the committees on the ministry of both or all presbyteries, with direct supervision of the person's ministry being given by the presbytery in which the licentiate is serving.

6.207 A licentiate who has been authorized to serve as a stated supply is nevertheless expected to continue his or her preparation for ordination.

6.208 A licentiate is not a member of presbytery or synod, and thus has no vote in these bodies; nor can a licentiate be a commissioner to the General Assembly.

6.209 A licentiate may be given a letter of dismission to another presbytery, but that presbytery is not bound to receive the letter. The receiving presbytery may give the licentiate the regular examination above stated. A licentiate must unite with a particular church in the presbytery to which he or she transfers.

6.210 A licentiate retains membership in a particular church. But inasmuch as such a person may perform certain functions of ministry only by authority of presbytery, he or she is subject to the disciplinary action of presbytery.

6.211 A presbytery may at any time drop the name of a licentiate from its roll, but not without indicating the reason therefor, nor without giving the licentiate an opportunity to be heard.

6.30 Ordination of Ministers

6.31 Ordination is the setting apart of a licentiate to the full work of the gospel ministry. Since the ordained ministry is the highest ecclesiastical office of the church, presbyteries shall be careful to ordain no one until fully satisfied with his or her qualifications for so important a work. A licentiate shall be ordained only if he or she has a call to a church or to a ministry approved by the presbytery. Presbyteries shall not feel obligated to ordain a licentiate because of long tenure as such, nor continue him or her longer than there is promise of usefulness.

6.32 Prior to ordination the licentiate shall sustain a careful and satisfactory examination by the committee on the ministry and the presbytery as a whole upon the following: experimental religion, continuing spiritual growth, the internal call to the ministry, knowledge of the scriptures, church history, systematic theology, pastoral care and counseling, church administration, the educational task of the church, preparation and delivery of sermons, the nature and meaning of public worship, and the doctrine and government of the Cumberland Presbyterian Church/Cumberland Presbyterian Church in America. As part of the above examination presbytery may require such written and spoken discourses as may be judged needful, including the planning and conducting of a presbyterial worship service with the licentiate delivering the sermon. The prior examination by the committee on the ministry shall not preclude examination by the presbytery.

6.33 In addition to the disciplines of study named above, presbytery shall encourage the licentiate as part of his or her preparation for ordination to obtain at least a working knowledge of the Hebrew and Greek languages, the usefulness of which to the understanding of the scriptures is hereby affirmed.

6.34 No licentiate shall be ordained who has not completed a degree in a graduate school of theology approved by the presbytery. Exceptions may be made only of persons possessing suitable gifts and abilities for a fruitful ministry, but who, because of reasons considered valid in the judgment of the presbytery, cannot be expected to complete the regular course of study in a graduate school of theology. In such cases a licentiate shall not be ordained until he or she has satisfactorily completed under the direction of the presbytery a two-year program of alternate studies approved by the General Assembly.

6.35 Ordination shall be by the presbytery at either a regular, an adjourned, or a called meeting; or it may be by a commission of the presbytery, which must consist of a quorum of the body and include two ordained ministers.

6.36 When a presbytery shall become satisfied with the qualifications of a licentiate, it shall announce a date and place for ordination and make preparation for the same. Following the sermon in a regular worship service at the time and place previously announced, the licentiate shall take his or her place at the front of the sanctuary. After a brief statement by the person presiding as to the purpose of the meeting and the meaning of ordination, the following questions shall be proposed to the licentiate:

I.   Do you believe the scriptures of the Old and New Testaments to be the inspired word of God, the authority for faith and practice?

II. Do you sincerely receive and adopt the Confession of faith of the Cumberland Presbyterian Church/Cumberland Presbyterian Church in America as containing the essential doctrines taught in the holy scriptures?

III. Do you approve of and promise to uphold the government of the Cumberland Presbyterian Church/Cumberland Presbyterian Church in America?

IV. In participating as a minister in the judicatories of the church, do you promise to share in a responsible way in the decisions that are made, to abide by those decisions, and to promote the welfare of the church?

V.   As far as you know your heart, have you been induced by the Holy Spirit to answer the call to the ministry from love of God and neighbor and a sincere desire to glorify God and advance his Kingdom in the world?

VI. As God may enable you, do you promise to be zealous and faithful in maintaining the truths of the gospel and the purity and peace of the church, irrespective of any opposition that may arise to you on that account?

VII. Do you promise to be faithful and diligent in the exercise of all your duties as a Christian and a minister of the gospel, and endeavor to so conduct yourself both privately and publicly as not to give offense to Christ and his church?

The above questions being answered in the affirmative, the licentiate shall kneel. All ministers of the presbytery present, with advisory members by invitation, and all elders who are members of the presbytery, shall gather around him or her. As the person presiding, or another appointed for the purpose, offers an appropriate prayer, all the presbyters shall, by the laying on of hands, solemnly set the licentiate apart to the office of the gospel ministry.

Then, with all the presbyters reverently standing, the person presiding shall say:

In the name of the Lord Jesus Christ, the great Head of the church, and by the authority of this presbytery, I now declare you duly ordained to the office of the gospel ministry, committing to you full authority to preach the word, to administer the sacraments, and to bear rule in the church.

Then the presiding minister, followed by all the presbyters, shall take the new minister by the hand, saying to him or her: We give you the hand of fellowship to take part in the ministry of the gospel with us.

After the presbyters have returned to their places, the person presiding, or some other person appointed for the purpose, shall deliver an appropriate charge to the new minister. A prayer shall then be offered in which the new minister is recommended to the grace of God for that ministry to which he or she has been set apart.

The transaction shall be duly recorded in the presbyterial minutes, the newly ordained minister's name added to the roll of ministers of the presbytery, and the church of which the minister was a member notified to drop his or her name from its roll.

6.40 Recognition of Ordination

6.41 A minister of another ecclesiastical body who desires to become a minister in the Cumberland Presbyterian Church/Cumberland Presbyterian Church in America shall appear before the committee on the ministry of the presbytery in which he or she wishes to be received. The committee on the ministry shall investigate the following:

a. Whether the minister has proper credentials from his or her ecclesiastical body;

b. Whether the minister has a degree from a college and graduate school of theology;

c. Whether the minister has a knowledge of the history, theology, and government of the Cumberland Presbyterian Church/ Cumberland Presbyterian Church in America;

d. Whether the minister seems fit for service as a minister in the Cumberland Presbyterian Church/Cumberland Presbyterian Church in America.

6.42 The committee on the ministry, if satisfied in each of the areas described in Section 6.41 may recommend to presbytery that the minister be received as an ordained minister in the Cumberland Presbyterian Church/Cumberland Presbyterian Church in America, upon giving affirmative answer to the questions put to licentiates at their ordination. Such procedure shall not exclude the opportunity for presbytery to examine the minister.

6.43 If the person seeking to become a minister in the Cumberland Presbyterian Church/Cumberland Presbyterian Church in America neither has degrees from a college and a graduate school of theology nor has completed a course of study comparable to the program of alternate studies approved by the General Assembly, he or she shall be required during a probationary period to meet the educational standards for ordination. A person who does not have a college degree or has not completed the program of alternate studies shall have the status of a candidate. A person who has a college degree or has completed the program of alternate studies required of a licentiate shall have the status of a licentiate. When the educational requirements have been satisfied, the probationary period may be ended and the minister's previous ordination confirmed upon giving affirmative answer to the questions put to licentiates at their ordination. Such procedure shall not exclude the opportunity for presbytery to examine the minister.

6.50 Jurisdiction over Ministers

6.51 A letter of dismission for a minister, licentiate, or candidate shall be granted to a particular presbytery of the Cumberland Presbyterian Church/Cumberland Presbyterian Church in America or another ecclesiastical body. A minister, licentiate, or candidate shall remain under the appropriate jurisdiction of the presbytery granting the letter of dismission until proper notification of reception by the presbytery or other ecclesiastical body to which the letter was granted. No minister, licentiate, or candidate of one presbytery shall be received by another presbytery of the Cumberland Presbyterian Church/ Cumberland Presbyterian Church in America without a duly certified letter of dismission from the former presbytery.

6.52 If a minister lives outside the bounds of the presbytery in which he or she desires to hold membership, he or she must receive the consent of the synod in which that presbytery is located to hold membership in that presbytery.

6.53 A minister against whom no charges are pending or who is under no disciplinary action, if fully satisfied that God has not called him or her to the ministry, or if he or she has satisfactory evidence of his or her inability to serve as a minister, or if he or she shall for any other reason desire to do so, may request that his or her ordination be revoked and that he or she be divested of the office. The committee on the ministry shall be directed to counsel with the person, if it has not already done so, and report to the next stated meeting of the presbytery. If the person remains firm in his or her request, the presbytery shall approve the request, noting that it is not a disciplinary action.

6.54 A minister whose ordination has been revoked at his or her own request or by deposition may be received as a member in a particular church on re-affirmation of faith.

6.55 A retired ordained clergy may, upon his or her retirement and request be thereafter excused from further meetings of the presbytery and synod without affecting his or her relationship to presbytery and synod.

7.00 RELATIONS BETWEEN MINISTERS, LICENTIATES, OR CANDIDATES AND CHURCHES

7.01 A person may be called to a particular church to one of four relationships: pastor, associate/assistant pastor, stated supply, or interim pastor.

7.02 The office of pastor is to be held only by an ordained minister, whom the particular church has called for an indefinite time and to whom the presbytery has entrusted the spiritual care of the church, including the office of moderator of the session.

7.03 The office of associate/assistant pastor is to be held only by an ordained minister whom the particular church has called for a definite or indefinite time to fulfill various pastoral functions as outlined by the church issuing the call, and approved by the presbytery. In the absence of the pastor, the associate pastor may, with the approval of the pastor and session, serve as moderator of the session or of a congregational meeting.

7.04   The office of stated supply may be held by an ordained minister, a licentiate, or a candidate, whom the particular church has called for an indefinite time, or, in the case of an interim supply, for a definite time, for less than full time work. An ordained minister serving as stated supply may fulfill all duties and functions pertaining to the spiritual care of the church, including moderating the session. A licentiate or a candidate serving as stated supply may fulfill the duties and functions except moderating the session, administering the sacraments, and solemnizing marriages.

7.05   The office of interim pastor is to be held by an ordained minister who is invited by the session of a church without an installed pastor. An interim pastor may preach the word, administer the sacraments, and fulfill pastoral duties for a specified period of time not to exceed twelve months, while the church is seeking a pastor. An interim pastor may not be called to be the next installed pastor or associate/assistant pastor of a church served as interim pastor.

7.06   A person shall enter into one of these relationships with a particular church only with the approval of the presbyteryin the bounds of which the particular church is located. The church session shall bear responsibility for the selection of the person, and the presbytery's approval shall relate to the person's ministerial credentials, commitment to the theology and government of the Cumberland Presbyterian Church/Cumberland Presbyterian Church in America, and standing in his or her current presbytery, if any. The presbytery may authorize its board of missions to act on its behalf in examining the call and to give tentative approval to a relationship between a particular church and a minister, licentiate, or candidate, subject to formal approval at a meeting of the presbytery.

7.07   The relationship between a minister, licentiate, or candidate and a particular church may be dissolved only by presbytery, acting on the request of both parties, or on the request of one party if sufficient reasons are presented, or when, in the opinion of the presbytery, the well-being of the particular church demands it.

7.10   Installation of Pastors and Associate/Assistant Pastors

7.11   Pastors and associate/assistant pastors shall be installed by presbytery or by a commission of presbytery. The service of installation shall include a sermon appropriate to the occasion, a brief explanation of the nature of the pastoral relation, and the asking of the following questions:

To the minister:

I. Are you willing to assume the responsibilities as pastor (or associate/assistant pastor) of this church, according to the agreements made in your acceptance of the call?

II. Do you believe that in taking upon you these pastoral responsibilities you are influenced by a sincere desire to promote the glory of God and the good of the church?

III. Do you solemnly covenant that, in reliance upon the grace of God, you will endeavor faithfully to fulfill the responsibilities of a pastor (or associate/assistant pastor) to this church, to preach and teach the word of God, to care for the sick, the troubled, the dying, and the bereaved, and to lead this church in its witness and ministry, as God gives you wisdom and strength?

When these questions have been answered in the affirmative, the following questions shall be asked:

To the elders of the session:

I. As the immediate representatives of the people, are you willing to share with the minister, as your pastor (or associate/assistant pastor), in the government and leadership of the congregation?

II. The Constitution identifies the session of a particular church as the minister in charge and the elders elected by the people. The session thus constituted is charged with the pastoral oversight of the congregation. Are you, with this minister in charge, willing to share fully in the pastoral oversight of the congregation?

III. Do you covenant with this minister, as your leader and pastor, to share openly and fully with him or her about all the ministries of this particular church, praying for and with him or her, and encouraging him or her in this work with you?

To the congregation:

I. Are you willing to enter into the pastoral relation with this minister whom you have called to be your pastor (or associate/assistant pastor)?

II. Do you covenant to encourage and assist him or her in the ministry which you share with him or her in this congregation?

III. Do you covenant that through your stewardship and prayers you will continue that material and spiritual support by which he orshe will be sustained in his or her ministry with you?

When these questions have been answered in the affirmative, the presiding minister shall say:

I now declare that _____ has been regularly called

and installed pastor (or associate/assistant pastor) of this congregation, agreeable to the word of God and according to the government of the Cumberland Presbyterian Church/Cumberland Presbyterian Church in America. Therefore, _____ is entitled to all support, encouragement, and honor in the Lord. In the name of the Father, and of the Son, and of the Holy Spirit. Amen.

The presiding minister, or one appointed for the purpose, shall then deliver an appropriate charge to the pastor (or associate/assistant pastor) and to the congregation to fulfill the covenant made between them. Then, by prayer, the minister shall commend them to the grace of God and to God's holy keeping.

8.0 SYNOD

8.1   A synod consists of at least three presbyteries in a prescribed area and the ministers and the elder representatives from the churches within those presbyteries.

8.2   Representation to synod may be based on either all ministers and the elder representative/s from each church within the presbyteries with one (1) elder representative from each church for every 300 active members or a portion thereof or designated representatives from each presbytery consisting of one (1) elder and one (1) minister for every 1,000 active members or a portion thereof within the presbytery; the elders being from different churches.

8.3   The synod having met at the time and place appointed may proceed to business provided a quorum of six persons (ministers and session representatives) are present, including at least one minister and one elder, with representation from at least three presbyteries.

8.4   Members of a presbytery from which an appeal or protest is made shall not be entitled to vote on that question.

8.5   A synod has the oversight and responsibility to:

a. Examine and decide appeals, protests, and referrals regularly sent up from the presbyteries;

b. Review the records of the presbyteries, redress whatever they may have done contrary to order, take effectual care that they observe the government of the church and obey the injunctions of the higher judicatories;

c. Organize, divide, or dissolve presbyteries, when deemed expedient;

d. Appoint persons to such work as may be under synod's jurisdiction;

e. Formulate budgets and assign shares to the presbyteries;
f. In general, to order with respect to the presbyteries, sessions, and churches under its care according to the government of the church, whatever pertains to their spiritual welfare and the edification of the church,
g. Settle differences regarding church property and its use, upon appeal;
h. Concert measures for promoting the prosperity and enlargement of the church within its bounds; and,
i. Propose to the General Assembly such measures as may be of common advantage to the entire church.

8.6   The synod shall keep full and accurate records of its proceedings, submit them to the General Assembly for review at its stated meetings, and in general, report on all important changes and the state of religion within its bounds, as well as supplying other information which may be requested by the General Assembly.

8.7   The synod shall meet as often as once every two years on its own adjournment, and when an emergency shall require a meeting sooner than the time to which it stands adjourned, the moderator, or in case of the moderator's absence, death, or inability to act, the stated clerk shall with written concurrence or at the written request of three minister members and three session members, with representation from at least three presbyteries, call a special meeting. The call shall give notice, specifying the particular business of the intended meeting, to every minister and session of every particular church on its roll, at least thirty days prior to the proposed time of meeting. Nothing shall be transacted at such a called meeting other than the particular business for which the synod was convened.

8.8   If, for any cause, the synod shall fail to meet according to its adjournment, it shall be the duty of the moderator, or, in case of the moderator's absence, death, or inability to act, the stated clerk, or, in case of the stated clerk's absence, death, or inability to act, persons constituting the equivalent of a quorum, to call a meeting as early as practical, at such place as may be designated, for the transaction of the regular business. For this purpose notice shall be given to every minister and session on its roll at least thirty days prior to the meeting.

9.0 GENERAL ASSEMBLY

9.1   The General Assembly is the highest judicatory of this church and represents in one body all the particular churches thereof. It bears the title of the General Assembly of the Cumberland Presbyterian Church/Cumberland Presbyterian Church in America and constitutes the bond of union, peace, correspondence and mutual confidence among all its churches and judicatories.

9.2   The General Assembly shall meet as often as once every two years, at such time and place as may have been determined, and shall consist of commissioners from the presbyteries in the following proportions:

FOR CUMBERLAND PRESBYTERIAN CHURCH

a. A presbytery having an active membership (including ordained clergy) of 1-1000 shall be entitled to send one minister and one elder;

b. A presbytery having an active membership (including ordained clergy) of 1001-2000 shall be entitled to send two ministers and two elders;

c. The basis for representation shall continue in the above proportions.

FOR CUMBERLAND PRESBYTERIAN CHURCH IN AMERICA

a. A presbytery having an active church membership of 1-200 shall be entitled to send one minister and one elder;

b. A presbytery having an active church membership of 201-400 shall be entitled to send two ministers and two elders;

c. A presbytery having an active church membership of 401-1000 shall be entitled to send three ministers and three elders;

d. A presbytery having an active church membership of 1001-above shall be entitled to send four ministers and four elders.

An elder must be serving as a member of a session at the time of the meeting of the General Assembly in order to be eligible to serve as a commissioner.

When an emergency shall require a meeting sooner than the time to which it stands adjourned, the Moderator, or in case of the Moderator's absence, death, or inability to act, the Stated Clerk shall with the written concurrence or at the written request of twenty commissioners, ten of whom shall be ministers and ten elders, representing at least five presbyteries, call a special meeting. The call shall give notice in writing at least sixty days prior to the proposed meeting, specifying the particular business of the intended meeting, to the stated clerks of all presbyteries, and to all commissioners and their alternates. Nothing shall be transacted at such a called meeting other than the particular business for which the General Assembly was convened.

9.3   Any twenty or more commissioners, of whom at least ten are ministers, and ten elders, being met on the day and at the place appointed shall be a quorum for the transaction of business.

9.4   The General Assembly has oversight and responsibility to:

a. Receive and decide all appeals, protests, and referrals regularly brought before it from the lower judicatories;
b. Bear testimony against error in doctrine and immorality in practice, injuriously affecting the church;
c. Decide in all controversies respecting doctrine, discipline, church property, and interpretation of the Constitution;
d. Institute and review the work of denominational entities;
e. Give its counsel and instruction in conformity with the government of the church in all cases submitted to it;
f. Review the records of the synods;
g. Take care that the lower judicatories observe the government of the church and exercise its review and appellate authority to redress what they may have done contrary to order,
h. Formulate budgets and assign shares to the presbyteries;
i. Concert measures for promoting the prosperity and enlargement of the church and create, divide, or dissolve synods;
j. Appoint persons to such labors as are under its jurisdiction;
k. Resolve schismatic contentions and disputations, according to the government and discipline of the church;
l. Receive under its jurisdiction other ecclesiastical bodies whose organization conforms to the doctrine and order of this church, and authorize synods and presbyteries to exercise similar power in receiving bodies suited to become constituents of those judicatories and lying within their geographical bounds, respectively;
m. Keep watch over the affairs of the whole church;
n. Correspond with other churches; and,
o. In general, recommend measures for the promotion of love, truth, and holiness throughout all the churches under its care.

9.5   The General Assembly, in order to promote the mission work of the Church and the development of new churches outside the United

States, may authorize a synod or its missions entity (utilizing ordained personnel) to act in place of a presbytery with respect to persons, ministers, and churches outside the United States and outside the bounds of any existing presbytery. The missions entity or synod may attach mission work to an existing presbytery, with the presbytery's approval. The General Assembly shall provide for the oversight and responsibility of the body's ecclesiastical actions.

9.6   If, for any cause the General Assembly shall fail to meet at the time and place to which it stands adjourned, it shall be the duty of the moderator, or, in case of the moderator's absence, death, or inability to act, the stated clerk, to call a meeting as early as practical, at such place as may be designated, for the transaction of the regular business. For this purpose notice shall be sent to the stated clerks of the presbyteries not less than sixty days prior to the meeting. In case of the absence, death, or inability to act of both the moderator and stated clerk, such meeting may, in like manner, be called by five commissioners, from any five of the presbyteries.

10.0 RELATIONS BETWEEN CHURCHES

10.1   The General Assembly, a synod, or a presbytery may cooperate with the General Assembly, a synod, a presbytery or a comparable judicatory of another ecclesiastical body or bodies, and a presbytery may authorize one or more of its constituent churches or agencies to cooperate with a church, churches, or agencies of another ecclesiastical body or bodies in undertaking and conducting a program. This may be done through informal arrangement or through formal structure, including incorporation.

10.2 When a particular church of another ecclesiastical body, whose constitution contains provisions similar to these, requests that it be received by a presbytery of this church, the presbytery shall not receive the particular church from the other ecclesiastical body unless:

 a. That particular church has been regularly dismissed by the presbytery or comparable judicatory of jurisdiction and any timely complaint to such action of dismissal has been finally determined; and

 b. Both the receiving and dismissing presbytery have sought the advice of the appropriate agency of the highest judicatory of their church dealing with relations between ecclesiastical bodies.

When a particular church has been properly dismissed and received under the above provisions, no financial consideration shall be required of the receiving presbytery except that if the property is encumbered by mortgage, or other encumbrance, the receiving presbytery shall assume and agree to pay all obligations of such encumbrance.

10.3 When a particular church of another ecclesiastical body with dissimilar constitutional provisions to these, or an independent congregation, requests that it be received by a presbytery of this church, the presbytery shall not receive the particular church unless:

(a)　That particular church has been regularly dismissed by a comparable judicatory, or is certified by congregational vote to be free to pursue a relationship with this church because it is self-determining, and there are no pending ecclesiastical or civil complaints against the congregation, and

(b)　The presbytery has investigated to assure that the congregation comes on good faith and desires to embrace Cumberland Presbyterian doctrine, polity, and practice, and will undergo mentoring, clergy and lay, for a provisional period of not less than two years.

During the provisional period, the congregation shall, under supervision of presbytery, operate as a Cumberland Presbyterian Church in all respects, and shall have official representation at presbytery. Members of the congregation will be eligible to serve on judicatory boards and as General Assembly Commissioners upon completion of the provisional period. If at any time during the provisional period either presbytery or the congregation is dissatisfied with the progress toward assimilation as a Cumberland Presbyterian Church, the relationship shall be dissolved thirty days after formal vote by the presbytery and/or congregation to that effect, with written notice of that intent to presbytery and the congregation.

10.4 A presbytery may authorize one or more of its constituent churches to form a federated or union church with a church or churches of another ecclesiastical body or bodies or may organize a federated or union church acting in concert with a comparable judicatory of another ecclesiastical body or bodies. This shall be done by agreement in writing between the presbytery and the comparable judicatory of the other ecclesiastical body or bodies.

10.5 A presbytery or synod of the Cumberland Presbyterian Church in America and a presbytery or synod of the Cumberland Presbyterian Church, whose boundaries coincide or can be made to coincide, may form a union presbytery or synod which shall be related in the same way to both denominations.

11.0 AMENDMENTS

11.1 Amendments to the Confession of Faith, Catechism, Constitution, Rules of Discipline, Directory for Worship, and Rules of Order may be proposed to the General Assembly of the Cumberland Presbyterian Church or the General Assembly of the Cumberland Presbyterian Church in America. If received favorably by either General Assembly, all proposed amendments shall be referred to a Joint Committee on Amendments composed of the five members of the Permanent Committee on Judiciary of each General Assembly for preparation for the two assemblies for action.

11.2 When a proposed amendment to the Confession of Faith, Catechism, Constitution, or Rules of Discipline is presented by the Joint Committee on Amendments to the General Assembly of each church, on recommendation of each assembly the amendment may be transmitted to its presbyteries by three-fourths vote of the members thereof voting thereon, provided there is present and voting not less than 75% of the full membership of the assembly based on the complete representation of all its presbyteries.

11.3 An amendment to the Confession of Faith, Catechism, or Rules of Discipline shall have been adopted when, on its transmission by both assemblies to their presbyteries, a three-fourths majority of the presbyteries of each General Assembly shall have approved it and such approval is declared by each General Assembly to have been given. The vote of a presbytery shall be by simple majority.

11.4 An amendment to the Constitution shall have been adopted:

a. For both churches, when a three-fourths majority of the presbyteries of each General Assembly shall have approved it and such approval is declared by each General Assembly to have been given; each presbytery voting by simply majority, and,

b. For either church when a three-fourths majority of its presbyteries shall have approved it and such approval is declared by its General Assembly to have been given; each presbytery voting by simple majority. In such instances the amendment shall be identified as applicable to the Constitution of the church adopting it, and the original section to which the amendment was applied shall remain a part of the Constitution of the church rejecting it.

c. Presbyteries shall act upon an amendment referred by the General

Assembly within the first year of the referral and report their vote no later than the next meeting of the General Assembly after the amendment was transmitted to the presbyteries.

11.5 An amendment to the Directory for Worship or the Rules of Order shall have been adopted when a two-thirds majority of the entire number of commissioners enrolled at each General Assembly shall have approved it, provided such amendment shall not conflict in letter or spirit with the Confession of Faith or Constitution.

APPENDICES TO THE CONSTITUTION
APPENDIX I
LETTER OF DISMISSION FOR CHURCH MEMBERS

(To be forwarded by the clerk of the session of the dismissing congregation to the proper official of the receiving church. Husband and wife should be issued individual letters.)

This certifies that _____, a member in good standing of the _____congregation of _____Presbytery of the Cumberland Presbyterian Church/Cumberland Presbyterian Church in America, is hereby dismissed at his/her own request to the _____ congregation of the _____ Church. The following are the names of his/her baptized children:_____.
The above named person is an elder □, deacon □, in the Cumberland Presbyterian Church/Cumberland Presbyterian Church in America.

Given by order of the session of the _____congregation of the Cumberland Presbyterian Church/Cumberland Presbyterian Church in America, this the _____ day of _____ AD _____.

Signed_____
　　　　　　(Moderator or Clerk of Session)
Address_____.

APPENDIX 2
CERTIFICATE OF RECEPTION FOR CHURCH MEMBERS

(The pastor of the receiving congregation should complete this form, detach, and mail to the moderator or clerk of the session granting the letter.)

This certifies that _____, a member in good standing of the _____ congregation of the Cumberland Presbyterian Church/Cumberland Presbyterian Church in America, upon presentation of a letter of dismission from the above named congregation, bearing the date _____, 20_____, was received by the _____congregation of the _____ Church on _____, 20____. Signed_____ (Pastor).

A permanent record of the dismissal should be kept by the clerk and should include the following:

Session Clerk's Record

Name of Member_____ Address_____
Dismissed to:
Name of congregation_____
Name of denomination_____
Letter of Dismission sent to: Name_____
Address_____ Datesent_____
Certificate of Reception returned: Date received_____

Note: If Certificate of Reception is not returned in six months inquiry should be made.

APPENDIX 3

ADMISSION OF NEW CHURCHES

When a new church is organized, the session shall apply for the new church's admission into the presbytery in whose bounds it is located. The following form may be used:

TO THE PRESBYTERY OF _____
The undersigned respectfully declare that on the _____
day of _____, AD _____, a new church was
organized at _____ by the Reverend
_____ (or a commission of presbytery),
which adopted the principles of the government of the Cumberland Presbyterian Church/Cumberland Presbyterian Church in America, and has a membership of _____. The following persons were elected as elders:_____, _____,
_____. The following persons were elected as deacons:_____, _____, _____.

We apply to be received under your care, and promise as the session to comply with all the duties and obligations enjoined upon particular churches and their officers by the government of the Cumberland Presbyterian Church/ Cumberland Presbyterian Church in America.

_____
_____
_____
Date_____   Elders

APPENDIX 4

SELECTING PASTORS AND ASSOCIATE/ASSISTANT PASTORS

In calling a minister to be the pastor or associate/assistant pastor of the church, the session should endeavor to ascertain the will of the membership, and should select the minister it believes will best serve the interests of that particular church. The call should be presented to the minister as follows:

_____Church,   being satisfied of your ministerial qualifications and being confident of your ability to minister to the diverse needs of this congregation extends to you a call to serve for an indefinite period of time as pastor (or associate/ assistant pastor) of this church and to join with us in a ministry to the entire community. We commit ourselves to provide the support, cooperation, and encouragement necessary to enable you to fulfill this calling. We pledge to pay an annual salary of $_____.

The call may then detail other considerations such as vacation arrangements, sick leave, travel costs in serving the congregation, and terms regulating the termination of the contract. The call in its entirety will be subject to the approval of the presbytery.

APPENDIX 5

LETTER OF DISMISSION FOR MINISTERS OR PROBATIONERS

(To be completed and forwarded by the stated clerk of the dismissing presbytery to the stated clerk or the proper official of the receiving judicatory.)

This certifies that _____
,
an ordained minister ☐ , licentiate ☐ , candidate ☐ , in good standing in the _____ Presbytery of the Cumberland Presbyterian Church/Cumberland Presbyterian Church in America, is hereby at his/her own request dismissed therefrom and is recommended favorably to the _____ Presbytery of the Cumberland Presbyterian Church/Cumberland Presbyterian Church in America, or to the following judicatory of the designated church: _____. Given by the order of _____
Presbytery, this _____ day of _____ A.D. _____.
Signed_____(Stated Clerk)
Address_____

APPENDIX 6

CERTIFICATE OF RECEPTION
FOR MINISTERS OR PROBATIONERS

(The stated clerk or the proper official of the receiving judicatory must complete this form, detach, and mail to the stated clerk of the dismissing presbytery.)

This certifies that _____

, an ordained minister □ , licentiate □ , candidate □ , of the Cumberland Presbyterian Church/Cumberland Presbyterian Church in America, upon presentation of a letter of dismission from the _____

Presbytery, bearing the date _____, 20____, was received by the _____ Presbytery of the Cumberland Presbyterian Church/Cumberland Presbyterian Church in America, or the following judicatory of the designated church: _____ on the date _____, 20____.

Signed_____(Stated Clerk or other authorized official)

Address_____

Presbyterial Clerk's Record of Dismission

Name_____, an ordained minister   □, licentiate □, candidate   □, was dismissed to the _____ Presbytery of the Cumberland Presbyterian Church/Cumberland Presbyterian Church in America, or the following judicatory of the designated church:_____ on the _____ day of _____ A. D. _____.

Record of Reception

The above named person was received by the _____ Presbytery of the Cumberland Presbyterian Church/Cumberland Presbyterian Church in America, or the following judicatory of the designated church: _____ _____ on the _____ day of _____ A. D. _____.

Record of the Reception signed by:_____

(Stated Clerk or other authorized official)

Address _____

RULES OF DISCIPLINE
1.0 PURPOSE OF DISCIPLINE

1.1   Discipline in the church is a positive expression in the spirit of love and helpfulness of concern both for the offender and for the church. Its purpose is that the life and work of the church may be orderly, conducive to the spiritual growth of the members, and corrective of weaknesses, mistakes and offenses by individuals and judicatories. Appropriate reasons for discipline are actions contrary to the faith and practice to which, according to the scriptures, all Christians are called, or which are contrary to the government of the church.

1.2   Discipline in the church should be appropriate to the nature of the error or offense. All acts of discipline, both for individuals and judicatories, should be weighed carefully, keeping in mind the purpose of discipline.

1.3   The various approaches in discipline have the same purpose and generally should begin with counseling and only then proceed to the more severe approaches. Discipline may include, but is not limited to, the following:

   a. Counseling is the effort to encourage and assist the person or judicatory to correct what is wrong, to remedy deficiencies, and to learn and grow spiritually through the experience;
   b. Admonition is a formal action to identify the weakness, mistake, or offense of a person or judicatory and to urge or order its correction;
   c. Suspension of a member of a church is a temporary exclusion from the right to vote in a congregational meeting and a removal from any position of leadership, including the session and diaconate. For a minister it is a temporary prohibition against the performance of the duties of the office. For a judicatory it is a temporary withdrawal of its power to act and a denial of representation in higher judicatories. Suspension may be for a definite or indefinite period of time;
   d. The act of deposing is the revoking of the ordination of a minister, elder, or deacon and removal from the office.

2.0 AUTHORITY IN DISCIPLINE

2.1   The responsibility and authority for discipline in a particular church belongs to the session. Oversight of the children of the church belongs first to their parents, but the session is responsible to give support to parents as they lead and guide children in their spiritual formation. The action by the session to admonish or suspend a member shall be taken only with respect to serious offenses, and then only after full opportunity is given for the approach of counseling. Removal of an elder from the session or a deacon from the diaconate may be accompanied by deposition from office.

2.2 The responsibility and authority for the discipline of ministers and churches rests with the presbytery to which they belong. The action by the presbytery to admonish, suspend, or depose shall be taken only with respect to serious offenses and then only after full opportunity is given for the approach of counseling.

2.3 When the action of a particular church is detrimental to the spiritual welfare of its members or to the connectional relations and ministries of the larger church, it shall be counseled by the board of missions of the presbytery or by a special committee or commission appointed by the presbytery. Should counseling fail to achieve the desired objective, the presbytery may admonish the church and instruct its session to correct what is wrong, suspend the session and govern the church temporarily through a commission, dissolve the session and conduct a new election of elders, or dissolve the church and attach its members to other congregations.

2.4 The responsibility and authority for discipline of their constituent judicatories by synods and the General Assembly is exercised in general review and control, or in response to an appeal of an action taken by a constituent judicatory. When the action of a constituent judicatory is contrary to the rules of government of the church or detrimental to the connectional relations or life and ministries of the church, it may be counseled through a special committee or commission, admonished, suspended, instructed to correct what is wrong, or dissolved.

2.5 Each presbytery shall have a standing commission which shall be called the "judiciary committee." Each judicatory above the session shall have a standing commission which shall be called the "disciplinary commission." Notwithstanding that these bodies may be called "committees," each of these standing commissions shall exercise the powers and responsibilities entrusted to it under these Rules, and shall be authorized to deliberate upon and conclude any business submitted to it pursuant to these Rules. A judicatory may assign other duties and responsibilities to its judiciary committee or its disciplinary commission, with or without the authority to act upon or to conclude such other the matters.

Comment: The judiciary committee and disciplinary commission may be separate bodies or may be subcommittees of existing committees or commissions of the judicatory. These bodies could also have responsibilities in addition to those assigned in these rules. In some instances, a committee may be a "hybrid" body, acting in some of its responsibilities as a committee and at other times acting with the authority of a commission. For example, a presbytery may already have a judiciary committee which performs other, committee-like functions. The judiciary committee can continue to perform its function as a presbyterial committee, exercising only the traditional role and authority of a committee. However, when the judiciary committee is performing a function under these disciplinary rules, it takes on the role of a commission and "shall be authorized to deliberate upon and conclude any business submitted to it." Because the judiciary committee and disciplinary commission may act as commissions, each should be composed of enough ministers and elders to constitute a quorum of the presbytery (or synod, as the case may be).

3.0 DISCIPLINE OF PERSONS

3.100 Cases Without Disciplinary Hearings

3.101 When a member, at his or her own initiative, acknowledges to the session an error or offense and gives evidence of a sincere effort to correct the matter, a record shall be made of the case. With the consent of the person, any disciplinary action taken shall be without a formal disciplinary hearing.

3.102 When a member in good standing without securing a letter of dismission or asking that his or her name be removed, shall join some other Christian church or religious body, the irregularity shall be noted and his or her name removed from the membership roll by action of the session. If there are charges pending against the person, or if he or she is under some disciplinary action, this information shall be communicated to the church or religious body upon its request. If the member is an elder or deacon, and he or she joins a religious body other than a Christian church, his or her ordination shall be revoked and he or she shall be divested of the office.

Comment: Paragraph 3.102 applies only if the member is moving to another denomination. If the member is joining another Cumberland Presbyterian church, the fact that charges are pending may, and generally should, be communicated to the new church. When the member is leaving the Cumberland Presbyterian denomination, information on charges pending against the member is provided only upon the request of the receiving church.

3.103   A minister, at his or her own initiative, may acknowledge to the judiciary committee an error or offense. If the minister gives evidence of a sincere effort to correct the matter and consents to any discipline proposed by the committee, the matter may be resolved and the discipline imposed without a formal disciplinary hearing. Otherwise, the judiciary committee shall refer the matter to the disciplinary commission for action as provided in section 3.400.

3.104   When a minister in good standing, without asking for a letter of dismissal, shall join some other Christian church or religious body, the irregularity shall be noted and his or her name removed from the presbyterial roll by action of the presbytery. If charges are pending against the person, or if he or she is under disciplinary action, this information shall be communicated to the church or religious body upon its request. If the minister joins a religious body other than a Christian church, his or her ordination shall be revoked and he or she shall be divested of the office.

Comment: Paragraph 3.104 applies only if the minister is moving to another denomination. If the minister is moving to another presbytery of the Cumberland Presbyterian church, the fact that charges are pending should be communicated to the new presbytery. When the minister is leaving the Cumberland Presbyterian denomination, information on charges pending against the minister is provided only upon the request of the receiving church.

3.200   Disciplinary Hearings Before Sessions

3.201   Any charges made against a member (the accused) shall be acted upon by a session only if they are in the form of a written document signed by the person making the charges (the complainant). The complainant may be a person who claims to be a victim of the conduct which is the basis for the complaint or another member who has reliable and compelling information about the conduct in the complaint. Whether or not the charges are written, the session or any of its members may counsel with a member to encourage and assist the member to learn and grow spiritually.

Comment: Disciplinary hearings for church members and for ministers are addressed in separate sections. Paragraph 3.201 makes it clearer that the charges may be brought, and the written charges can be signed, by a person other than the victim of the misconduct. For example, written charges can be brought by a witness to the misconduct or someone in whom the victim has confided (such as a parent) if there is "reliable and compelling information" that misconduct has occurred. The paragraph also reminds sessions that Christian counseling is always in order.

3.202   No charges against a person shall be considered if they are made more than two years after the alleged error or offense, except in the case of sexual misconduct or sexual harassment, in which case a ten (10) year time limit shall apply, but in the case of the sexual abuse or molestation of a child, no time limit shall apply.

3.203   When a session has received charges affecting the Christian character of a person under its care, it shall designate a committee to investigate the charges and counsel with the person accused. If the charges concern matters of potentially serious consequences, the session may at any time suspend the person from any position of leadership until the conclusion of the hearing and of any appeals. It shall be stated that the suspension is not a presumption of guilt but is a measure needed for the welfare of the church.

3.204   If the committee reports that, upon investigation, it finds no basis for the charges, the session shall dismiss the charges. If the committee finds that there are grounds to believe that an offense was committed by the accused, and the accused acknowledges the error or offense, and gives evidence of a sincere effort to correct the matter, the committee shall so report to the session and recommend appropriate disciplinary action. With the consent of the person, disciplinary action may be imposed without a formal disciplinary hearing. A record shall be made of the case, and the moderator shall direct the clerk to notify the complainant of the discipline imposed.

3.205   If the committee, upon investigation, finds that there are grounds to believe that an offense was committed by the accused, but the accused has not acknowledged the error or offense, or does not consent to the proposed disciplinary action, the committee shall present a written report to the session which includes a statement of the charges, the information the committee obtained in its investigation, the committee's findings, and its recommendations for discipline. The session shall hold a hearing to determine guilt, to impose discipline, or both.

a. Unless the accused, the complainant, and the session agree otherwise, a date for the hearing shall be set no sooner than ten (10) days. The moderator shall direct the clerk to give written notice of the hearing to the person charged (the accused); the person filing the charges (the complainant); all active members of the session; the investigating committee; and all witnesses requested by the accused, the complainant, or the session. The notice shall include the statement of the charges as framed by the investigating committee and shall state that the decision to conduct the hearing is not an indication that the accused is guilty of the offense.

b. Written notice should be hand delivered or sent by first class mail to the last known address of the person entitled to notice. Written notice provided in some other manner is effective if actually received.

c. The session may postpone the hearing for good cause. The failure of the accused or the complainant to appear at the hearing shall not automatically cause a postponement.

3.206 The hearing shall be conducted as follows:

a. The hearing shall be a closed meeting unless the accused, the complainant, and the session agree otherwise. If closed, the persons permitted to attend shall be: the members of the session; the accused and a companion; the complainant and a companion; and, if requested by the session, a representative from the investigating committee. The session shall determine whether to permit all of the witnesses to be present for the entire proceeding or to hear witnesses one at a time.

Comment: The "companion" who is permitted to accompany the complainant or accused may be a spouse, parent, other family member, friend, or a professional adviser such as a counselor or attorney. However, unless the companion is also a witness, he or she has no role in the process except to provide support and advice to the complainant or accused. The companion should not inject himself or herself into the proceedings. If the companion is an attorney, he or she should bear in mind that the proceeding is an ecclesiastical or spiritual proceeding, not a legal one.

b. The clerk shall keep a complete recording of the hearing, either by audio recording, audio-video recording, or by a written transcript.

   c. The moderator shall charge the members of the body and all others present to remember the purpose of discipline in the church as stated in Section 1.1.

   d. The statement of charges prepared by the investigating committee shall be read.

   e. The list of witnesses shall be reviewed. Any person may challenge whether a witness is competent to provide evidence. The session shall be the final judge of whether a witness is competent to provide evidence and whether any evidence offered is relevant to the proceeding.

   f. The accused may give a statement in response to the charges.

   g. Testimony and other evidence against the accused shall be received first, followed by testimony and other evidence on behalf of the accused. Testimony should be offered in a manner consistent with the purposes of discipline, and not in a bitter or retaliatory spirit.

   h. The moderator shall provide an opportunity for the accused, the complainant, or members of the session to question each witness and any other evidence. The moderator may disallow any question which is frivolous, irrelevant, or otherwise inappropriate, but the moderator's ruling may be appealed to the session.

   i. The accused or the complainant may challenge the right of any member of the session to speak or vote on the grounds of personal prejudice, including undue personal interest in the matter. All challenges shall be decided by the session.

   j. A final statement may be made by the complainant and the accused, who shall have the right to speak last.

   k. Only the members of the session shall be present during, and participate in, the deliberation of the case. All of the evidence shall be weighed and evaluated.

   l. The session shall vote on the following question: "According to the evidence presented, is it more likely that the accused is guilty or not guilty of the charge(s) made against him or her?" The accused shall be found not guilty unless a majority of those members of the session who are present and voting shall find the accused guilty.

3.207 If the accused is found not guilty:

a. The moderator shall announce the decision to the accused and the complainant. The moderator shall remind those present of the gravity of disciplinary proceedings, the nature of the church as a fellowship of reconciliation, and the responsibility of all Christians to act toward each other in the spirit of repentance and forgiving love.

b. No record of the charges or the decision need be entered into the minutes unless the session, for good cause, shall direct otherwise.

3.208 If the accused is found guilty:

a. The session shall determine the discipline under which he or she shall be placed. When the nature of the discipline has been determined, the moderator shall announce the decision and the discipline to the accused and the complainant. Any discipline imposed shall take effect immediately unless the session directs otherwise.

b. The moderator shall urge the person placed under discipline to respond to the decisions in prayer and self-examination and to make such efforts as are possible to remedy the error or offense.

c. The moderator shall remind those present of the gravity of disciplinary proceedings, the nature of the church as a fellowship of reconciliation, and the responsibility of all Christians to act toward each other in the spirit of repentance and forgiving love.

d. The minutes shall reflect the name of the accused, the charges of which he or she has been found guilty, and the discipline imposed. Appropriate care shall be taken to protect the name or identity of any victim.

3.209 If, after a disciplinary hearing has been held, new evidence is discovered that could alter the decision that was made, the person under discipline may ask the session to conduct a supplemental hearing. If the session determines that a new hearing should be held, only evidence not already presented may be offered at the new hearing.

3.210 If there appears to be sufficient evidence to warrant terminating the discipline imposed, the session may conduct a hearing to consider such action. The discipline may be terminated if sufficient and reliable testimony or other evidence is presented that (i) the person has repented of the error or offense; (ii) the person has taken steps to correct the matter; and (iii) the session finds that the person is unlikely to commit the error or offense again.

Comment: Discipline should not be terminated unless the session believes it is unlikely that the person will commit the error or offense again.

3.211 When a person under some kind of discipline moves his or her membership to another church, the session may, if it seems advisable, transmit a summary of the disciplinary hearing to that body, which shall proceed to act as though it had imposed the discipline.

3.300   Specific Procedures for Elders and Deacons
3.301   No elder or deacon, because of the office, is to be shielded from investigation or discipline; nor is he or she, because of the prominence which the office gives, to be subjected to investigation on insignificant charges nor disciplined on slight grounds.

3.302   If, as a result of an investigation and hearing as provided in section 3.200, an elder or deacon has been found guilty of an error or offense that has caused great harm in the church or seriously compromised his or her ability to perform the duties of the office, regardless of any mitigating circumstances, he or she shall be suspended or deposed. The session shall nevertheless express its hope that healing and reconciliation may be accomplished.

3.303   When an elder or deacon has been suspended or deposed, the session shall continue to exercise pastoral care over the person, with the particular intention of bringing about reconciliation and restoration.

3.304   When an elder or deacon is suspended or deposed, or when the suspension or deposition has been removed, notice of the action shall be given to the congregation.

3.305   When an elder or deacon has been deposed, the action to remove the discipline renews the ordination and restores the office, but in order to serve in a congregation the person must be elected again.

3.400   Discipline of Ministers
3.401   A complaint of misconduct on the part of a minister should be reported to the stated clerk of the presbytery or a member of the disciplinary commission. The person who receives the complaint shall promptly communicate it to the chair of the disciplinary commission and the stated clerk.

Comment: These rules recognize an important philosophical principle regarding a complaint: Once a complaint has been made, jurisdiction over the complaint belongs to the body (in this case, the presbytery or its subordinate bodies), and not to the individual who initially brought the complaint. A complaint will not result in a formal disciplinary hearing if the disciplinary commission, upon investigation, finds the complaint to be groundless. Conversely, if it appears that a member of the presbytery has engaged in misconduct, it is the duty of the presbytery, not the complainant, to see that the misconduct is stopped and appropriate discipline is imposed. These rules place the burden of going forward on a complaint on the disciplinary commission and the judiciary committee, not on the complainant. Any person with knowledge of a complaint should assist the complainant in getting the complaint to the attention of the proper authority.

3.402 Any charges made against a minister (the accused) shall be acted upon by the disciplinary commission only if they are in the form of a written document signed by the person making the charges (the complainant). The complainant may be a person who claims to be a victim of the conduct which is the basis for the complaint or another person who has reliable and compelling information about the conduct in the complaint. Whether or not the charges are written, the disciplinary commission or any other member of a presbytery may counsel with a minister to encourage and assist the minister to learn and grow spiritually.

3.403 No charges against a minister shall be considered if they are made more than two years after the alleged error or offense except as provided below. In the case of sexual misconduct or sexual harassment, the charges must be brought within ten (10) years after the alleged error or offense. In the case of the sexual abuse or molestation of a child, no time limit shall apply.

3.404 When the disciplinary commission has received charges affecting the Christian character of a person under the care of the presbytery, it shall investigate the charges and counsel with the minister accused. If the charges concern matters of potentially serious consequences, the disciplinary commission may at any time place limitations on the person's ministry or suspend the person from any position of ministry until the conclusion of the hearing and of any appeals. It shall be stated that the action taken is not a presumption of guilt but is a protective measure for the welfare of the church.

3.405 If the disciplinary commission, upon investigation, finds no basis for the charges, it shall close the matter and report that action to the accused, the complainant, and the judiciary committee. If the committee finds that there are grounds to believe that an offense was committed by the accused, and the accused acknowledges the error or offense and gives evidence of a sincere effort to correct the matter, the disciplinary commission shall so report to the judiciary committee and recommend appropriate disciplinary action. With the accused's consent, the judiciary committee may impose disciplinary action without a formal disciplinary hearing. A record shall be made of the case, and the committee on ministry shall notify the complainant of the discipline imposed.

3.406 If the disciplinary commission, upon investigation, finds that there are grounds to believe that an offense was committed by the accused, but the accused has not acknowledged the error or offense, or does not consent to the proposed disciplinary action, the disciplinary commission shall name from one to three of its members to serve as representatives to bring the charges before the judiciary committee in a formal hearing. The disciplinary commission shall promptly provide a written report to the chair of the judiciary committee which includes the names of the commission's representatives, a statement of the charges, the information the commission obtained in its investigation, the commission's findings, and its recommendations for discipline.

3.407 The judiciary committee shall hold a hearing to determine guilt, to impose discipline, or both.
a. Absent extraordinary circumstances, the hearing shall take place no sooner than fourteen (14) days nor more than thirty (30) days from the date the disciplinary commission makes its report. The chair of the judiciary committee shall give written notice of the hearing to the accused; the complainant; the members of the judiciary committee; the representatives of the disciplinary commission; and all witnesses requested by the accused or representatives of the disciplinary commission. The notice shall include the statement of the charges as framed by the disciplinary commission and shall state that the decision to conduct the hearing is not an indication that the accused is guilty of the offense.
b. Written notice should be hand delivered or sent by first class mail to the last known address of the person entitled to notice. Written notice provided in some other manner is effective if actually received.
c. The judiciary committee may postpone the hearing for good cause. The failure of the accused or the complainant to appear at the hearing shall not automatically cause a postponement.

3.408 The hearing shall be conducted as follows:
a. The hearing shall be closed except to those persons entitled to notice of the hearing. The judiciary committee may determine whether to permit all of the witnesses to be present for the entire proceeding or to hear witnesses one at a time.
b. The judiciary committee shall keep a complete recording of the hearing, either by audio recording, audio-video recording, or

by a written transcript.

c. The hearing shall be conducted by the chair of the judiciary committee or, if the chair is absent, by the vice chair or another member of the judiciary committee. The chair shall charge all those present to remember the purpose of discipline in the church as stated in Section 1.1.

d. The statement of charges submitted by the disciplinary commission shall be reviewed.

e. The list of witnesses shall be reviewed. Any person may challenge whether a witness is competent to provide evidence. The judiciary committee shall be the final judge of whether a witness is competent to provide evidence and whether any evidence offered is relevant to the proceeding.

f. The accused may give a brief statement in response to the charges.

g. Testimony and other evidence against the accused shall be received first, followed by testimony and other evidence on behalf of the accused. Testimony should be offered in a manner consistent with the purposes of discipline, and not in a bitter or retaliatory spirit;

h. The chair shall provide an opportunity for the accused, the representatives of the disciplinary commission, or members of the judiciary committee to question each witness and any other evidence. The moderator may disallow any question which is frivolous, irrelevant, or otherwise inappropriate, but the chair's ruling may be appealed to the judiciary committee.

i. The accused or the representatives of the disciplinary commission may challenge the right of any member of the judiciary committee to speak or vote on the grounds of personal prejudice, including undue personal interest in the matter. All challenges shall be decided by the judiciary committee.

j. A final statement may be made by the representatives of the disciplinary commission and/or the complainant and the accused, but the accused shall have the right to speak last.

k. Only the members of the judiciary committee shall be present during, and participate in, the deliberation of the case. All of the evidence shall be weighed and evaluated.

l. The judiciary committee shall vote on the following question: "According to the evidence presented, is it more likely that the accused is guilty or not guilty of the charge(s) made against him or her?" The accused shall be found not guilty unless a majority of those members of the judiciary committee who are present and voting shall find the accused guilty.

3.409   If the accused is found not guilty:

a. The chair shall report the decision to the accused, the complainant, and the representatives of the disciplinary commission. The chair shall remind those present of the gravity of disciplinary proceedings, the nature of the church as a fellowship of reconciliation, and the responsibility of all Christians to act toward each other in the spirit of repentance and forgiving love.

b. The judiciary committee shall make a report to the presbytery as follows: "The judiciary committee considered charges brought against [name of accused]. After an investigation and hearing, the committee found [name of accused] not guilty of the charges."

3.410   If the accused is found guilty:

a. The judiciary committee shall determine the discipline under which he or she shall be placed. If the error or offense has caused great harm in the church and seriously compromised his or her ability to perform the duties of the office, regardless of any mitigating circumstances, he or she shall be suspended or deposed.

b. When the nature of the discipline has been determined, the chair shall announce the decision and the discipline to the accused, the complainant, and the representatives of the disciplinary commission. Any discipline imposed shall take effect immediately unless the judiciary committee directs otherwise.

c. The chair shall urge the minister placed under discipline to respond to the decisions in prayer and self-examination and to make such efforts as are possible to remedy the error or offense.

d. The chair shall remind those present of the gravity of disciplinary proceedings, the nature of the church as a fellowship of reconciliation, and the responsibility of all Christians to act toward each other in the spirit of repentance and forgiving love.

e. The judiciary committee shall make a report to the presbytery in a closed meeting attended only by the committee and the members of presbytery, except that the complainant and the accused shall have the opportunity to address the presbytery in the meeting. The report shall include the name of the accused, the charges of which he or she was found guilty, and the discipline imposed. Appropriate care shall be taken to protect the name or identity of any victim.   The action of the judiciary committee shall be final unless the presbytery, by a two-thirds vote shall appoint a new commission to review the finding of guilt, the discipline imposed, or both. If a new commission is appointed, it shall review the decision of the judiciary committee using the rules applicable to an appeal.

Comment: There are several reasons why a two-thirds vote of the presbytery is required to overturn the decision of the judiciary committee.   The presbytery has vested its authority in the judiciary committee.   Rescinding the committee's decision is treated like a motion to rescind, which requires a two-thirds vote (see Rules of Order sec. 8.35b).   Most presbyteries have considered it wise not to address disciplinary matters on the floor of presbytery for several reasons (including the press of time, the need to protect a victim's privacy, concern about defamation or other legal liabilities, and the fact that, especially for larger presbyteries, presbyterial meetings do not lend themselves well to conducting hearings).   An appeal can proceed directly to the next highest judicatory without the delay inherent in waiting for the presbytery to meet.

3.411   If, after a disciplinary hearing has been held, new evidence is discovered that could alter the decision that was made, the minister under discipline may ask the judiciary committee to conduct a supplemental hearing. If the judiciary committee determines that a new hearing should be held, only evidence not already presented may be offered at the new hearing.

3.412   No minister, because of the office, shall be shielded from investigation or discipline; nor shall he or she, because of the prominence which the office gives, be subjected to investigation on insignificant charges nor disciplined on slight grounds.

3.413   If a minister habitually fails to engage in some form of ministry approved by the presbytery as described in the Constitution, it shall be the duty of the presbytery to inquire into the reasons for such failure and to take such action as may be proper.

3.414   When a minister has been suspended or deposed, the presbytery shall continue to exercise pastoral care over the person and shall confer with the person about his or her continuing church relation.

3.415   A minister who has been suspended or deposed may be restored only at his or her request. If there appears to be sufficient evidence to warrant restoring the minister, the judiciary committee may conduct a hearing to consider such action. The minister may be restored only if the judiciary committee finds on the basis of sufficient and reliable testimony or other evidence that (i) the person has, over a satisfactory period of time, exhibited repentance for the error or offense; (ii) the person has taken steps to correct the matter; (iii) the person is unlikely to commit the error or offense again; and (iv) the person is fit for ministry in the Church. Restoring a minister who has been deposed renews his or her ordination and restores the office.

3.416 When a minister is suspended he or she shall not perform the duties of the office in any church during the time of suspension. Any church which he or she is serving as pastor shall be notified of the suspension. Any church, aware of the suspension, and which permits the minister to perform the duties of the office in its bounds during the time of suspension, becomes liable to discipline.

3.417 When a minister is suspended, the presbytery may, at its discretion, dissolve the pastoral relationship which he or she has with any church in its bounds.

3.418 When a minister is deposed he or she shall not perform the duties of the office in any church. Any church which he or she is serving as pastor shall be notified, and the presbytery shall dissolve the pastoral relationship. Any church which is aware of the act of deposing, and which permits the minister to perform the duties of the office in its bounds, becomes liable to discipline.

3.419 When a minister has been suspended or deposed, the clerk shall send a notice to the clerks of all other presbyteries stating that the person was found guilty of a serious error or offense and deposed. When a minister has been restored, the clerk shall send a notice to the clerks of all other presbyteries stating that the person has been restored.

3.500 Appeals Regarding the Discipline of Persons

3.501 An appeal of a disciplinary action removes the case to the next higher judicatory. An appeal of any disciplinary action of a lower judicatory must be filed within thirty (30) days after the decision of the session, the presbytery's judiciary committee, or the synod's judiciary committee, whichever shall apply. If no appeal of a judicatory's action is filed in a timely manner, the action of the lower judicatory shall be final.

Comment: An appeal may be filed long before the disciplinary action has been reported to the full presbytery or synod. If the presbytery or synod votes to reconsider the disciplinary decision which has been made on its behalf, the appeal is dismissed in order to give the lower judicatory the opportunity to make a final decision. Once an appeal has been decided by a higher judicatory, it is too late for the lower judicatory to undertake a reconsideration of its own decision.

3.502 If a lower judicatory whose action is being appealed votes to reconsider its decision, the appeal shall be dismissed and the matter sent back to the lower judicatory. When the lower judicatory has completed its reconsideration and taken a final action on the matter, that action may be the subject of a new appeal.

3.503 Proper grounds for appeal are: the lower judicatory failed to follow the proper procedures; the lower judicatory committed an error or injustice in the decision; or the lower judicatory acted contrary to the Constitution or other rules of the church.

3.504 An appeal of a matter regarding the discipline of persons may be made by the complainant or an accused who has been found guilty of an offense or error. A disciplinary decision of a presbytery's judiciary committee may also be appealed by the presbytery's disciplinary commission.

3.505 An appeal is begun by filing a notice of appeal with the stated clerk of the next higher judicatory. The notice of appeal shall include information sufficient to identify the person making the appeal, the body which issued the ruling from which the appeal is taken, the grounds for the appeal, and that portion of the decision below which is being appealed.

3.506 The stated clerk shall promptly forward a copy of the appeal to the chair of the judicatory's standing judiciary committee. The appeal shall go forward unless the stated clerk and the chair of the judiciary committee find that the appeal fails to meet the criteria for a proper appeal, in which case the appeal shall be dismissed. If the appeal is dismissed, the stated clerk shall write a letter to the person who filed the appeal explaining why the appeal was dismissed. If the appeal is permitted to go forward, the chair of the judiciary committee shall obtain the record of the full hearing held by the session or the judiciary committee, whichever shall apply.

3.507 The proper parties to an appeal are as follows:

a. In an appeal from the action of a session, the accused and the complainant.

b. In any other appeal, the accused, the complainant, and the presbytery's disciplinary commission.

c. The party which files the appeal shall be the appellant, and all other parties shall be considered respondents.

3.508 The appeal shall be considered by the judiciary committee of the higher judiciary, which shall hold an appeal hearing as soon as practical after the receipt of the appeal.

a. Written notice of the appeal hearing shall be provided to the accused, the complainant, the presbytery's disciplinary commission, and the members of the judiciary committee hearing the appeal. The notice shall include the date, time, and place of the appeal hearing; the names of the accused and the complainant; the statement of the charges which were the subject of the hearing below; the decision reached by each lower judiciary which has considered the matter; the name of the party who appealed; the grounds for the appeal; and describe the portion of the decision below which is being appealed.

b. Written notice should be hand delivered or sent by first class mail to the last known address of the person entitled to notice. Written notice provided in some other manner is effective if actually received.

c. The judiciary committee may postpone the appeal hearing for good cause. The failure of any party to appear at the hearing shall not automatically cause a postponement.

3.509 The appeal hearing according to the following rules.

a. The judiciary committee shall review the record of the hearing below, either during or shortly before the appeal hearing.

b. The judiciary committee shall hear first from the appellant, who shall explain why the action of the lower judiciary was flawed or incorrect. The judiciary committee shall then hear from the respondent or respondents. The appellant shall then be entitled to make a closing statement.

c. The appeal hearing shall be conducted entirely on the record of the proceedings below unless the judiciary committee shall request additional evidence or information. The appeal hearing may be continued in order that the additional information or evidence may be obtained.

d. Only the members of the judiciary committee shall be present during, and participate in, the deliberation of the appeal.

3.510 The judiciary committee shall rule against the appeal unless the appellant shows both:

a. the lower judiciary failed to follow the proper procedures; committed an error or injustice in the decision; or acted contrary to the Constitution or other rules of the church; and

b. the improper action by the lower judiciary had a significant affect on the final decision in the case.

3.511 If the judiciary committee rules against the appeal, the ruling of the lower judiciary shall stand. The appellant shall have a right of appeal to the next higher judicatory, if any.

3.512 If the judiciary committee rules in favor of the appeal, it may reverse the action appealed in whole or in part; remit the case to the lower judicatory for the purpose of amending an incorrect or defective record; or direct the lower judicatory to reconsider the action appealed.

3.513 The judiciary committee shall make a report directly to its judicatory which states: that an appeal was made, the parties to the appeal (except that appropriate care shall be taken to protect the name or identity of any victim), the grounds for the appeal, and the disposition of the appeal. The judiciary committee's disposition of the appeal shall be final unless the judicatory, by a two-thirds vote, shall appoint a new commission to review the appeal. If a new commission is appointed, it shall review the decision of the lower judicatory using the rules applicable to an appeal.

Comment: Because the judiciary committee's action is the act of a commission, the report of its action should go directly to the judicatory and should not pass through or be made to a committee of the judicatory.

4.0 DISCIPLINE OF JUDICATORIES

4.001 Every decision made by any judicatory, except the General Assembly, is subject to review by the next highest judicatory and may be brought before it by general review and control, appeal, or protest.

4.002 Persons who are members of a judicatory whose actions are the subject of appeal or protest shall not be eligible to serve on a committee or commission of the higher judicatory dealing with the appeal or protest; nor shall such persons, if members of the higher judicatory, be eligible to vote on any motions related to the appeal or protest.

4.100 General Review and Control

4.101 Every judicatory above the session shall, at stated intervals as prescribed, review the proceedings of the judicatory next below. If any judicatory shall fail to send its records to the next highest judicatory for this purpose, it may be ordered to do so immediately or on a specified date, or else face disciplinary action.

4.102 In reviewing the records of a lower judicatory, it is proper to

examine whether:
  a. The proceedings have been correct;
  b. The proceedings have been wise and equitable and for the edification of the church;
  c. The proceedings have been correctly recorded; and
  d. The directives of the higher judicatories have been obeyed.

4.103 Generally, the higher judicatory shall record in its minutes the approval of the record or any action it considers appropriate with regard to any errors or irregularities that were found. It shall make an entry of the same in the records under review. In addition, if any action is taken, it shall send a communication to the clerk of the judicatory whose records were under review, listing the errors or irregularities and indicating the corrective action that is to be taken. In reviewing the record of disciplinary actions against persons, no action of a lower judicatory shall be altered or reversed, unless regularly brought up by appeal.

4.104 Should a judicatory neglect to perform its duty, and thereby allow false doctrine or immorality to develop, offenders to go undisciplined, or other great irregularities to occur and not be properly recorded, the higher judicatory being aware by other means that such neglect or irregularity has occurred, shall make inquiry into and shall examine, deliberate, and decide the entire matter as if it had been recorded, and thus brought up by review and control.

4.105 When a judicatory has been advised by the records of a constituent judicatory, by resolution, or by any other satisfactory means of any important neglect, error, or irregularity of its proceedings, it may cite the lower judicatory to appear through a representative or in writing to explain what it has done or failed to do in the matter in question. Except in disciplinary cases, after full investigation the actions of a lower judicatory may be reversed in part or as a whole; or the matter may be referred back to the lower judicatory with instructions that it be reconsidered and corrective action taken. If the explanations of the lower judicatory are satisfactory and it is able to show that the matter is not of serious consequence, the review may be terminated with a caution to exercise greater care in future actions.

4.200 Appeals

4.201 The following rules apply to appeals of a disciplinary action by a judicatory concerning a constituent body and appeals of all non-disciplinary actions. An appeal removes a case already decided from a lower to the next higher judicatory.

4.202 Proper grounds for appeal are: the lower judicatory failed to follow the proper procedures; the lower judicatory committed an error or injustice in the decision; or the lower judicatory acted contrary to the Constitution or other rules of the church.

4.203 An appeal is begun by filing a written notice of appeal with the stated clerk of the next higher judicatory. The notice of appeal shall include information sufficient to identify the person(s) or judicatory making the appeal, the action which is being appealed, the judicatory which took the action which is being appealed, the grounds for the appeal, and that portion of the action below which is being appealed. Notice of appeal by a person or persons must be given within ten days of the action being appealed. Notice of appeal by a judicatory must be given within sixty days following the date of the action it wishes to appeal.

4.204 An appeal of a disciplinary action by a judicatory of one of its constituent judicatories may be made by any member of the higher judicatory, provided it is signed by one-third of those present and voting when the disciplinary action was taken; or it may be authorized by an action of the judicatory that is the subject of the discipline. The appeal suspends the disciplinary action until the appeal is finally decided.

4.205 An appeal of any and all non-disciplinary actions of a judicatory may be made by any person who is a member of the Cumberland Presbyterian Church/Cumberland Presbyterian Church in America, but it shall not suspend the action until the appeal is finally decided, except in the following cases, and then only if the appeal is signed by one-third of the members of the judicatory who were present and voting at the time the action was taken:

a. The ordination of a minister;
b. The action of a presbytery to unite, divide, or dissolve particular churches;
c. The action of a synod to unite, divide, or dissolve any of its presbyteries.

4.206 The proper parties to an appeal are as follows:

a. The person(s) or judicatory which filed the appeal, which shall be the appellant.
b. The judicatory which is alleged to have committed the error or offense, which shall be the respondent.

4.207 If the appeal has been properly and timely made, an appeal hearing shall be held as soon as practical after the receipt of the appeal. The appeal hearing shall be conducted by the higher judicatory or by a commission it appoints for that purpose.

a. Written notice of the appeal hearing shall be provided to the appellant, which shall be directed to the stated clerk if the appellant is a judicatory; to the stated clerk of the respondent; and to the members of the judicatory or commission which is hearing the appeal. The notice shall include the date, time, and place of the appeal hearing and shall include a copy of the notice of appeal filed by the appellant.

b. Written notice should be hand delivered or sent by first class mail to the last known address of the person entitled to notice. Written notice provided in some other manner is effective if actually received.

c. The judicatory or commission hearing the appeal may postpone the appeal hearing for good cause. The failure of any party to appear at the hearing shall not automatically cause a postponement.

4.208 The appeal hearing shall be conducted according to the following rules.

a. The judicatory or commission hearing the appeal shall confirm that the appeal was properly and timely filed.

b. The record of the action being appealed shall be reviewed.

c. The appellant (or a representative of the appellant if the appellant is more than one person or a judicatory) shall be called upon to explain the error or offense of the lower judicatory. The respondent shall have an opportunity to defend the action, or failure to act, of the lower judicatory. The appellant shall then be entitled to make a brief closing statement.

d. The body hearing the appeal may request additional evidence or information. If necessary, the appeal hearing may be continued in order that the additional information or evidence may be obtained.

e. Only the members of the judicatory or commission hearing the appeal shall participate in the deliberation of the appeal.

4.209 The appeal shall be denied unless the appellant shows the lower judicatory failed to follow the proper procedures; or committed an error or injustice in the decision; or acted contrary to the Constitution or other rules of the church.

4.210 If the appeal is denied, the action of the lower judicatory shall stand. The appellant shall have an immediate right of appeal to the next higher judicatory, if any. If the appellant fails to pursue another appeal in a timely manner, the appeal shall be regarded as abandoned and the action or decision appealed from shall be final.

4.211 If the judicatory or commission hearing the appeal rules in favor of the appeal, it may reverse the action appealed in whole or in part; remit the case to the lower judicatory for the purpose of amending an incorrect or defective record; or direct the lower judicatory to reconsider the action appealed. If the action of the lower judicatory is of such a nature that it cannot be corrected, the lower judicatory may be admonished.

4.300 Dissents and Protests

4.301 A dissent is a declaration unaccompanied by reasons by one or more members of a minority of a judicatory, expressing a different opinion from that of the majority as to a particular matter. If stated in temperate language, the dissent shall be noted in the records of the judicatory, together with the names of the persons dissenting.

4.302 A protest is a declaration accompanied by reasons by one or more members of a minority of a judicatory, expressing a different opinion from that of the majority, as to a particular matter. If stated in temperate language, the protest with its reasons shall be entered in the records, together with the names of the persons protesting.

4.303 When a protest is lodged by any member of a judicatory, the judicatory may respond to the reasons given in the protest.

4.304 The higher judicatory shall take cognizance of all protests appearing upon the records passing under its review. The higher judicatory may, but need not, take any other action with respect to a protest.

DIRECTORY OF WORSHIP

Preface

Worship is fundamental to the mission of the Christian church. To worship God is to act out our obedience to the God who has revealed himself to us, called and claimed us as his people. In worship the initiative lies with God and the focus is on God. God and God's redemptive and creative work are both the object and the subject of worship. To worship is to re-enact the gospel in its fullness and simplicity.

In worship we discover and express our identity as God's people, we participate in the ongoing redemptive work of God in the world and we offer ourselves anew to the One who has created, redeemed and sustained us. We worship because of who we are and who God is.

The dominant character of Christian worship is praise of God. Because of who God is, what God has done, and what God has promised to do, it is in order for us to praise God for that steadfast love which is peculiar to God.

Christians worship in the name of Jesus Christ: in the power of Jesus Christ and in the freedom of Jesus Christ. Jesus through his birth, life, death and resurrection offered up perfect worship to God, and as Christians we are free to participate in that perfect expression of praise. Therefore, the life and ministry of Jesus Christ is central to Christian worship, and all Christian worship seeks to reflect and be shaped by that life and ministry. Jesus Christ is the living Word whose presence and spirit alone make valid all of Christian worship.

As human beings we also realize that we worship out of a sense of need. We are not sufficient unto ourselves, and we experience a sense of completeness and fulfillment through the encounter with and worship of our Creator. To worship is to be fully human.

Christians can worship God at any time, for all time has been redeemed by him in Jesus Christ. From the beginning of Christian worship, however, one day has been set aside for corporate worship: the Lord's Day. This day is the first day of the week and it was designated as the proper day for corporate worship of Christians because it was the day Jesus Christ was raised from the dead. It was "on the first day of the week" that the followers of Jesus discovered the empty tomb and met the risen Lord. Hence the day appointed for Christian worship is a remembrance of the resurrection of Jesus. Each Sunday is understood by Christians at worship to be an Easter day; every time of corporate worship is understood to be a celebration of the victory of God acted out through the resurrection of Jesus the Christ.

The Lord's Day also commemorates the first day of creation. On the first day of the week God began creation, and likewise on the first day of the week God began his "new creation." Hence this day is seen as being basic to all good. God created the world and pronounced it good; in Jesus Christ God redeemed the world and claimed it anew for its goodness. Christians worship on the Lord's Day remembering and celebrating God's creation and redemption: God's creating the world and proclaiming it good and God's decisive action in making all things new and good. By designating one day as the Lord's Day Christians show forth what is true for all days and all creation: Jesus Christ is Lord of all creation.

I. THE CORPORATE WORSHIP OF GOD

God through Jesus Christ redeems individuals into relationship to himself and to one another as members of the church, which is the body of Christ. Christian worship, therefore, above all is to be understood as communal or corporate. This means that one's individuality finds its true meaning as a part of the community of faith and that individual worship is never understood to be in isolation from the faith and praise of the community. Moreover, it is in order to emphasize that individual or private worship is an essential part of the Christian life and is needful in order for corporate worship to find its deepest meaning and fullest integrity, just as corporate worship is necessary in order that individual worship can have appropriate substance and shape.

The corporate worship of the church also gives direction, focus and shape to the worship carried out by families. Their worship is guided by corporate worship and they are aware that their worship is done as people who are members of a worshiping community. Indeed, worship in the home is strongly encouraged. Scripture, prayer, hymns and personal witness are all a vital part of the worship of families.

A. THE ORDERING OF CORPORATE WORSHIP

It is appropriate that groups of Christians give thought to the ordering of their worship. Order and design are necessary not simply because worship is a social act in which agreed upon procedures are critical for responsible action by any group, but because God chose a specific form through which he carried out his ultimate act of self-revelation: the incarnation, the cross, the resurrection and the ascension of Jesus

Christ.

Throughout the history of the Christian movement order and design have been critical for corporate worship. Moreover, through the years a certain basic shape and design for corporate worship has emerged and has been adopted by Christians under the leadership of the Holy Spirit. This basic design has had at its center the praise and prayers of the people of God, the proclamation of God's Word and the celebration of the sacraments. These emphases in turn have been given particular order and expression so that a distinctive liturgical drama has been developed which is comprised of various components and actions in relationship to each other and to the overall purpose of worship.

Even so, there is no one "right" or "perfect" order or design for corporate worship. Rather, those designing corporate worship are to take thought for what is appropriate for a particular group on the basis of their specific situations together with the purpose and intent of the church's worship, and the liturgical tradition of their ecclesiastical body.

Corporate worship is always to be viewed as the people's service. The worshipers are not to be spectators watching what a few do, but participants who, together with those leading worship, are engaged in a mutual act of meeting between God and his called-out people. Leaders of worship should also keep in mind that they are worshipers too, and that their function is to enable all present to worship God.

The ordering of worship is not intended to prohibit spontaneity in corporate worship. Instead it is proper to design worship in anticipation of spontaneity. A variety of responses meaningful for the worshipers can be incorporated in the people's worship, and genuine, natural expressions of praise and confession are to be encouraged.

The Cumberland Presbyterian Church/Cumberland Presbyterian Church in America has never adopted any official liturgy. The responsibility for designing corporate worship for groups of Christians is lodged with the judicatories. In the case of the local congregation, it is the session, under the leadership of the pastor, who has responsibility for the design of corporate worship. The members of the other judicatories are responsible for ordering corporate worship for those groups of Christians, which at any given time are under the jurisdiction of that particular judicatory.

Ministers of the Word have special responsibilities for the ordering of corporate worship. They are educated in the history and theology of Christian worship and they are expected to give strong guidance and leadership to all persons who are engaged in designing and leading corporate worship.

B. ORDINARY ACTS OF CORPORATE WORSHIP

Persons designing and participating in corporate worship are to take thought for those acts which Christians historically have found to be valid and necessary expressions of their worship. These acts help us to remember and to understand what we are to do and what we are to say as we meet to worship God.

1. *Praise of God.* Worshiping God involves praising God. Christians praise God for who God is and for what God has done, is doing and has promised to do. We praise God because God is the Sovereign Lord over all of life.

2. *Confession of Sin.* While Christians are redeemed and worship as a part of the redeemed community, sin is still a part of their lives. Corporate worship has traditionally provided an occasion when Christians acknowledge their sinfulness and confess their sins to God.

3. *Proclamation.* Whenever Christians worship, the gospel is to be proclaimed. The gospel means good news and is centered in what God has revealed to humankind throughout history, especially God's ultimate revelation in Jesus Christ. In worship Christians both announce and hear that good news of God's love, grace, judgment, reconciliation, forgiveness, mercy, and God's gracious call to service.

4. *Affirmation of Faith.* Stating what the community of faith believes is an ordinary part of Christian worship. That faith both shapes the life of the worshipers and gives expression to the hope and expectancy which is a part of the Christian life.

5. *Offering.* The worship of the people of God is incomplete without the act of giving. Surely it is well to be reminded that in worship God gives himself anew to the worshipers. Also, in worship those present offer themselves to God, to be shaped, empowered, directed, changed by God; and they offer their gifts to God to be blessed and used by God.

6. *Commitment and Commissioning.* Corporate worship never loses contact with the world. In corporate worship the worshipers give thought for all the world, and are enabled to move into the world to serve God and participate with God in the ongoing redemption of the world. In corporate worship persons may respond in acts of repentance and faith and commit themselves to serve God and to serve other human beings in the name of Jesus Christ. It is fitting that acts of commitment and commissioning be included in worship.

7. *Celebrating the Sacraments.* The sacraments of the Lord's Supper and baptism are sign-acts of God's self-giving which are means by which God's grace is made available to us. The sacraments give a peculiar shape to the worship of Christians and are the primary signs of

the covenant of grace.

While it is appropriate to include all these acts in any occasion of corporate worship, it is not necessary to incorporate all acts in order to express valid worship. Over a period of time, however, all of the acts mentioned above should be expressed, and thought should be given by those responsible for designing corporate worship to ensure that such is so.

C. BASIC RESOURCES FOR CORPORATE WORSHIP

The resources used by those designing worship are to be tested for suitability by the purpose and intent of worship itself. Historically the resources used by the church are as follows:

1. *Scripture.*   Scripture is the written word of God and has a preeminent place in all aspects of the lives of Christians and the life of the church.

The reading of one or more passages of scripture should be a part of every corporate worship experience.

Those responsible for reading scripture in worship are expected to be very familiar with the selected passages and read them in such a manner that they are readily heard by the other worshipers. Scripture readings should be selected so that over a period of time the entire witness of scripture is read as a part of worship.

In addition to the reading of the Bible in worship, scripture is also the fundamental resource for the opening sentences or call to worship, the invitation to celebrate the sacraments, the assurance of pardon, the blessing, prayer, and proclamation. Indeed, scripture itself proclaims God's word.

2. *Prayers.*   Prayer is inseparable from the Christian life. To be a Christian is to pray and to join others in prayer. Prayer therefore is an essential aspect of all Christian worship.

Christians pray not primarily to "receive" something from God, but as an expression of their creaturehood and their dependence upon God as their creator. The primary purposes of prayer are: (1) to enter into the presence of God to experience anew God's judgment, grace and power; (2) to praise God, and (3) to invite God into our world and into our lives.

All prayer in corporate worship is informed by the Lord's Prayer. Its customary use as a vital part of worship is encouraged, and the nature and character of that prayer should serve as a guide for all prayer.

Christians also have the prayers that have been handed down through the church's history to use in corporate worship and to use as a guide for all prayers prayed in worship. The prayers of the "great cloud of witnesses" which surround us are our prayers, too, and enable all the saints, living and dead to participate in corporate worship.

It is in order to formulate new prayers for worship which are based upon and added to this prayer tradition. But whether new prayers are formulated or ancient prayers prayed anew, the matter of first importance is that they be in accord with the prayer tradition of the church.

Whether prayers are written or not is of no prime importance. What is important is that ordinarily the prayers be prepared and that they be prayed so that all present may participate in the prayers.

Prayer involves, among other emphases, the following: adoration or praise of God, confession of sin, offering of thanksgiving, interceding on behalf of others, supplication and surrender, offering of ourselves and our gifts.

3. *Music.* The earliest records of the Christian community make clear that music was an integral part of the worship of believers. Singing their praise and prayers was customary and meaningful.

Music enables worshipers to offer their worship in a more complete way. It is imperative therefore that music provide the occasion for people to focus upon God and God's will, to experience the presence of God and to worship God in spirit and truth.

Selection of music is to be done with utmost care, giving thought to the quality of the music, and its appropriateness for Christian worship and for the particular worshipers.

4. *Hymns, Spirituals and Gospel Songs.* Throughout the ages Christians have sung their faith as a part of their worship. Hymns, spirituals and gospel songs vary in content and focus and may be used as a part of the many different acts of worship: praise, confession of sin, proclamation, commitment, affirmation of faith.

From these resources for worship, care should be taken to ensure that the text expresses some aspect of biblical truth, and that the tune reflects music quality and is suitable for the people who are to sing it.

5. *Sermon.* In corporate worship the sermon is central to proclamation. Its purpose is to present some aspect of the gospel in a manner which will enable all present to be engaged once more by God's good news, have their lives claimed anew by God and invite a response of obedience to God's call.

Sermons are based upon scripture and shaped by scripture. In preparing sermons it is necessary to be guided by all of scripture in order that all aspects of the gospel will be proclaimed. Orderly selection of scripture passages upon which those preaching base their sermons, such as some form of lectionary, is encouraged.

Sermons should be preached in a manner which reflects informed communication skills.

6. *Creeds.* Creeds are one form of expressing what the community of faith believes. The Bible contains numerous creedal statements which summarize the faith of various worshiping groups. Scripture passages such as Deuteronomy 6:4-5, Deuteronomy 26:5-9, I Corinthians 15:3-7, Philippians 2:6-11 represent creedal statements likely used in corporate worship.

The ancient creeds known as the Apostles' Creed and the Nicene Creed still serve worshipers well. In addition, other creeds have been produced which may be used in worship as a means of expressing personal and corporate faith. It is appropriate for Christians to write new creeds for worship, so long as they are in accord with the biblical witness.

D. SUGGESTED ORDERS FOR CORPORATE WORSHIP

While there is no one order for worship which is appropriate for all Christians, there is a classic shape to corporate worship which informs all our worship. That shape is one of God's action and our response to God. The following orders for Christian worship are informed by that classical shape. The first order includes the celebration of the Lord's Supper, since the Lord's Supper is an act which gives the peculiar shape to all Christian worship.

1. Corporate Worship Including the Lord's Supper

Prelude

The corporate worship begins as Christians present themselves to join together to worship God. The music chosen for a prelude should enable people to focus their attention on God and God's kingdom. Worshipers are to be instructed that the prelude is a part of their corporate worship. It is not a "mood setter" or a time to "get ready" for worship. Perhaps ringing a bell before the prelude begins, or some signal from the leader of worship prior to the prelude indicating that worship is now to begin would be helpful. The liturgist may simply say "Let us worship God." Then the prelude can begin.

Opening Sentences

Traditionally these sentences have always been scripture with the focus being on God and our relationship to him. The classic model for Presbyterian worship has been Psalm 124:8, "Our help is in the name of the Lord who made heaven and earth." Many other passages of scripture can be used as opening sentences, and may be said responsively. But whatever passages are used, they will emphasize why the participants have gathered and what they are about. The use here of any material other than scripture should be carefully examined as to substance and intent.

Hymn of Praise

The dominant purpose of Christian worship is praise--the joyful response of the people to God's unspeakable gift in Jesus Christ. It is highly appropriate, therefore, that the people sing their praise to God following the opening sentences. The hymn should be one whose tune and text point to God's greatness, majesty, love and goodness.

Prayer of Adoration

Ordinarily the prayer following the hymn of praise continues the theme of praise and adoration. Care should be taken to shape the prayer as one of adoration, and remember that other prayers in the service will be shaped by other appropriate prayer emphases.

Confession of Sin and Declaration of Pardon *or Words of Assurance*

The confession of sin and the assurance of forgiveness are an integral part of worship, just as they are an integral part of the Christian life. Historically this act is found in one of two places: following the act of adoration or before the celebration of the Lord's Supper.

It is in order to call the worshipers to confession through the use of scripture passages. The prayer of confession follows and often it is most meaningful when prayed in unison. If it is prayed by one person on behalf of all, it should be carefully planned and thoughtfully prayed so that it can indeed be a corporate prayer in which all may participate.

The act of confession is to be followed by a strong affirmation or declaration of pardon. Here again scripture provides the best treasury for such affirmation, and needs no comment of any kind. For example, I John 1:9 is often used: "If we confess our sins, God is faithful and just, and will forgive our sins and cleanse us from all unrighteousness."

Responses of Praise

A response of praise appropriately follows the act of confession and the granted forgiveness from God. This response can take several forms. Psalms and canticles (songs from the Bible other than those contained in the Psalter) have long been used for this purpose. The reading from the Psalter is appropriately followed by the singing of the Gloria Patri ("Glory Be to the Father"), or some other response of praise.

The Hearing of God's Word

The reading, proclaiming and hearing of God's word constitute the second major movement in the order of worship. We gather to hear God's word addressed to us through the reading of scripture and the preaching of the sermon. Here proclamation is central and uppermost.

The reading of scripture is of critical importance to proclamation. Whoever is responsible for reading it should be adequately prepared and possess the ability to read well.

In selecting the scripture passage or passages to be read careful thought is to be given to providing the worshipers with all the many and varied themes and emphases of God's word.

The use of a lectionary for corporate worship is highly recommended. A lectionary is a systematic ordering of scripture to ensure that the many themes of scripture will be read and provide the basis for proclamation. Traditionally lectionaries are developed around the Christian year and prescribe specific readings for each Sunday. It is also appropriate for those who design worship to produce a lectionary for use.

Customarily the reading of scripture is preceded by a *Prayer for Illumination* which calls upon God to enable us to be receptive to his word.

It is appropriate that the scripture readings be separated by an *anthem* or *canticle* or *hymn*.

The *sermon* appropriately follows the last scripture reading and ordinarily is to be based upon one or more of the readings. Care should be exercised that the sermon not violate the integrity of worship nor compromise the biblical witness. A prayer or *Ascription of Praise* appropriately follows the sermon.

Affirmation of Faith or Creed

The affirmation of faith by the worshipers has from the early years of the Christian movement been a central part of corporate worship. Historically the recital of the Creed or personal *Affirmation of Faith* was the basis on which worshipers were admitted to the Lord's Supper. Only those persons who were willing to say "I believe..." were allowed to participate in the worship of the people of God at the table. Also, the *Creed* or *Affirmation of Faith* functions as a response to our hearing of God's word.

It is fitting also that an appropriate hymn be sung to express further the worshipers' belief or faith.

The Prayers of the People

The people's *Affirmation of Faith* is appropriately followed by the *Prayers of the People*. These are prayers that may be offered by a minister or a layperson to which all present can respond by saying "Amen."

The *Prayers of the People* may include thanksgiving, supplication, intercession, and conclude with the Lords' Prayer. Thanksgiving lifts up the expression of gratitude common to all those present and may include appreciation for the church; supplication focuses on the needs of the worshipers both individual and corporate; intercession incorporates the needs of those not present but whose needs are well known, especially the needs of those who are not members of the Christian community; the Lord's Prayer is the model of all our prayers and enables all present to pray according to Jesus' teaching and understanding of prayer.

The Presenting of the Gifts or Offering

Historically the offering was the occasion in corporate worship when the elements of bread and wine which were to be used in the Lord's Supper were presented. It is appropriate to bring them to the communion table still, or if the table has already had the elements placed upon it, they are at this time prepared for the Lord's Supper which is to follow.

At this point in the service, money and other offerings are brought forward. The giving of money is to be seen as an act of worship, a symbol of our commitment as individuals and as a corporate body to the redemptive work of God in the world. Even if there is no money to be given as a part of a particular service of corporate worship, some act of self-giving is in order for that service. The Doxology may be sung as an act of praise following the giving of our gifts, and the act of giving may conclude with a *Prayer of Dedication*.

The Celebration of the Lord's Supper

The celebration of the Lord's Supper is central to Christian worship.

In this liturgical act a visible presentation of the word is joined to it and proclamation. Together, sermon and sacrament bear witness to God's redemptive actions in the death and resurrection of Christ. It is always appropriate to include the sacrament as a part of corporate worship.

In celebrating the Lord's Supper, those designing worship should be guided by the acts which have traditionally accompanied that necessary part of corporate worship. Those acts may be identified by different names and be clustered under different headings, but essentially they are these:

  a. *Invitation to the Lord's Table.* The minister who is to lead the congregation in celebrating the Lord's Supper invites all who believe in Jesus Christ as their Lord and Savior to participate in this celebration.

  b. *Words of Institution.* Scripture passages which establish the warrant for this celebration are read or recited by the one who is designated to officiate at the communion table. Appropriate words are found in I Corinthians 11:23-26; Matthew 26:26-30; Mark 14:19-26, and Luke 22:19-20. Other passages of scripture which relate Jesus' meeting with his disciples for a meal after the resurrection may also be used for this purpose.

  c. *Prayer of Thanksgiving.* This prayer most often includes an expression of thanksgiving to God for who he is and what he has done in Jesus Christ, a calling upon God to send the Holy Spirit upon the elements and the people, and an offering of the lives of the people to be used by God.

  d. *Breaking and Pouring.* Action at this point in the liturgy is most meaningful. The acts of breaking the bread and pouring the wine dramatically remind us that Christ's body was broken and his blood was shed for all. It is important therefore that such action be thoughtfully done and clearly visible to all present. A loaf of bread of sufficient size needs to be provided for the breaking, and a chalice and flagon are necessary for the pouring. After the pouring, the chalice can be elevated for all to see. If the act of pouring is omitted, the chalice may still be elevated.

  e. *Partaking of the Elements.* Different ways of distributing the elements have developed in the life and worship of the church which are appropriate. Congregations of the Cumberland Presbyterian Church/Cumberland Presbyterian Church in America have traditionally followed the procedure of serving the worshipers in their pews. Using this method, the minister may partake of the elements, then serve the ruling elders, who in turn serve the congregation; or the minister and ruling elders may serve others first and then serve one another.

Another method used is having the members of the congregation come forward to partake and be served by the minister and ruling elders. Still another approach is to have the worshipers come forward and be served while seated at a table.

In each method used, worshipers may stand, sit or kneel.

Many worshipers have found the use of one loaf of bread and one cup (traditionally called the "common cup") for all worshipers to be most meaningful. Some congregations use the common cup only for the minister and the ruling elders.

f. *Post Communion Prayer.* A prayer of praise, commitment and intercession may follow the distributing of the elements. A canticle of the church or a hymn may appropriately follow this prayer.

g. *The Dismissal/Charge/Benediction.* Corporate worship may conclude with a dismissal signaling the concluding of worship, or a charge in which the people are exhorted to go into the world to be the people of God, or a pronouncement of a blessing upon the people, or any combination of the three. Leaders are encouraged to use biblical material for this act.

Postlude

Like the prelude this music should be chosen with corporate worship in mind. Moreover, if it is to be a part of worship, then all present should be requested to remain silent and listen to the postlude and make it a part of their worship. If this is to happen, it means that in most instances the postlude will be brief. If the postlude is not to be understood as a part of worship, then it is recommended that it be removed from the order of worship and that the service conclude with the dismissal or benediction.

Announcements

Persons responsible for designing corporate worship will need to think through how the making of necessary announcements will relate to corporate worship. Some congregations will choose to present all necessary announcements in a bulletin and expect the worshipers to read them without any mention of them being made as a part of worship. Other congregations may decide to make announcements *prior* to the beginning of corporate worship. Another option is to make announcements after corporate worship.

Those congregations which decide it is the wise choice to make announcements as a part of worship should give thought to how this can be done without disrupting worship. One possibility is to make announcements just prior to the *Prayers of the People*, and incorporate the concerns of the announcements into the prayers.   Whenever announcements are made as a part of corporate worship, they should be restricted to announcements which relate directly to the on-going mission of the congregation and have relevance for all members of the worshiping community.

2. An Order for Corporate Worship Without the Lord's Supper

Prelude
Opening Sentences
Hymn of Praise
Call to Confession
Declaration of Pardon
Psalter Reading
Gloria Patri
Prayer for Illumination
First Scripture Reading
Sermon
Ascription of Praise
Creed
Hymn
The Prayers of the People
The Offering
Offertory Anthem
Prayer of Dedication
Hymn
Benediction

3. A Second Order for Corporate Worship Without the Lord's Supper

Prelude
Opening Sentences or Call to Worship
Prayer of Adoration
Hymn of Praise
Prayer of Confession
Assurance of Pardon

Responsive Reading
Gloria Patri
Invitation to Give
Giving of Offering
Doxology
Prayer of Dedication
Prayer for Illumination
Scripture Reading(s)
Prayers of the People
Sermon
Hymn of Consecration
Benediction
Silent Prayer
Postlude

4. A Third Order for Corporate Worship Without the Lord's Supper

Prelude
Opening Sentences or Call to Worship
Processional Hymn
Prayers: Adoration (the people standing)
          Confession (the people seated)
Assurance of Pardon
Psalm
Gloria Patri
Scripture Reading(s)
Anthem
Sermon
Creed
Offering
Prayers of the People
Lord's Prayer
Recessional Hymn
Dismissal and/or Benediction
Postlude

E. ORDERS FOR OCCASIONAL WORSHIP

There are various occasions other than the Lord's Day when groups of Christians gather to worship. Families are encouraged in worship, different meetings and programs appropriately include worship, and through the week opportunities may be given for Christians to join together to pray and praise God. The following orders, or some adapted versions of them, are recommended for voluntary use.

Order 1
Prelude
Scripture Sentences
Hymn
Responsive Reading
Gloria Patri
Scripture Reading
Prayers
Hymn
Benediction
Postlude

Order 2
Scripture Sentences
Hymn of Praise
Confession of Sin
Assurance of Pardon
Doxology
Scripture Reading
Special Music
Prayers
Hymn
Silent Reflection
Charge and Dismissal

Order 3
Prelude
Opening Sentences or Call to Worship
Hymn
Scripture Reading
Silent Reflection on Scripture, or
Brief Interpretation of Scripture
Prayers
Hymn
Closing Prayer

Order 4
Hymn
Reading of Scripture
Brief Interpretation of Scripture
Silent Prayer
Lord's Prayer
Dismissal and/or Benediction

F. LEADERSHIP OF CORPORATE WORSHIP
General Guidelines
Thoughtful, responsible and imaginative leadership is critical for corporate worship; weak, careless and sloppy leadership diminishes significantly the worship of the people of God. The purpose of the leadership is to enable the worshipers to unite in their praise and homage to God, to act out the liturgical drama, and to respond obediently to God's claim on their lives. The leader directs the people with respect to actions or words.

There is no *one* way worship is to be conducted; the leadership will depend greatly upon the situation and the person or persons responsible for the leadership. The general rule for leadership is to do and say whatever is necessary to enable the worshipers to be certain what action is to take place or what is to be said, but do no more than is necessary. Some additional guidelines for leaders of worship are:

a. Present yourself as a worshiper along with the others;
b. Avoid any action or comment which primarily calls attention to yourself as a leader or distracts people from their worship;
c. Be direct and forceful in your leadership;
d. Plan carefully all comments and leadership actions;
e. Be brief and clear with all directions;
f. Learn how to lead non-verbally, and
g. Make use of the historically liturgical language in directing or leading the worshipers.

While the ordained minister is frequently the person most active in leading corporate worship, leadership of the worshipers is in no way restricted to the clergy. Various members of the congregation may function as leaders of worship and are encouraged to do so. The choir and instrumental musicians provide leadership for the parts of the worship involving music, and other laypersons also provide various types of leadership. It is paramount, however, that anyone who functions as a leader of worship be carefully prepared.

Symbols and Vestments

Through the centuries the Christian community has made use of symbols and vestments to aid in their worship. Christians can choose from this vast storehouse of symbols or create their own for use in the place designated for worship. What is crucial in use of symbols is that those who are asked to use them understand clearly their meaning and their function.

Vestments worn by leaders of worship may also enrich and enhance corporate worship. Robes worn by choir members and other musicians, clergy robes, albs, chasubles, stoles can all serve a useful purpose if they are properly introduced and understood. Vestments can fittingly symbolize the function of the leader of worship and can direct attention away from the individual to the responsibility the person is carrying out on behalf of the worshiper.

G. THE CHOIR, MUSICIANS AND CORPORATE WORSHIP

The primary choir for all singing in worship is the worshiping congregation. Where there is an auxiliary choir to provide liturgical leadership, the members of that choir should always understand themselves as worshipers offering their special gifts to God so that the congregation can sing and worship more faithfully. When a choir sings responses or anthems, it is representing the congregation, just as ordained ministers do when they pray or preach.

Choir directors and other musicians have knowledge concerning music which is valuable in planning and conducting corporate worship. They should work closely with ministers and others in designing the worship service. Ministers and musicians especially should work creatively with each other, sharing knowledge and understanding and learning from each other.

H. THE CHRISTIAN YEAR AND CORPORATE WORSHIP

As worship developed in the Christian community during the first centuries, an ordered attempt was made to ensure that in its worship the church would represent the whole of the gospel and the full spectrum of Christian truth. This ordering became known as the Christian year. The primary emphases of the Christian year are the birth, passion and resurrection of Jesus Christ, and the empowering of the church for mission. Various "seasons" (designated days or weeks) were developed so that suitable attention could be given to the various aspects of the gospel.

Worshipers are encouraged to be instructed by the seasons and emphases of the Christian year in order that their worship may more nearly reflect the whole of the gospel.

II. THE SACRAMENTS

Baptism and the Lord's Supper, the two sacraments instituted by Christ, are part of the full expression of corporate worship. They are understood to be signs of Christ's presence with us and thereby belong to the regular worship of Christians. The primary importance in both sacraments is what God does and the reality of God's self-giving in and through the water, bread and wine. Like all aspects of worship they are corporate acts in the deepest sense, and they always point to the saving grace of Christ and Christ's benefits offered to us. Especially do the sacraments re-enact the redemptive acts of God by which we are united to Jesus Christ and made one in Christ.

The power and meaning of the sacraments depend upon the presence of Jesus Christ, the incarnate Word. They are also linked to the proclaimed word, and are inseparably connected to the Word, incarnate and proclaimed. They are in a true sense a visible Word. The Word and sacraments together give the fundamental shape to all Christian worship.

A. THE SACRAMENT OF BAPTISM AND CORPORATE WORSHIP

Baptism is a sign of God's love for us and of Christ's grace extended to us. In baptism God claims persons as his own and marks them as peculiarly his, heirs of the covenant of grace. Baptism signifies and represents the forgiveness of sin, the engrafting into Christ, the coming of the Holy Spirit into our lives, and the death and resurrection to new life. It is both proclamation and affirmation. It proclaims that God's grace and love reach out to people before they are able to respond, and it affirms our new identity as members of the body of Christ. It sets people apart from the rest of the world, and claims them as participants in the ministry of Jesus Christ.

No person is worthy by her or his own merit to receive the gift of God's grace conferred and proclaimed in baptism. Whether it is a believer who is baptized or a child of a believer, each is totally dependent on God's grace and forgiveness freely offered in Christ through his church.

Baptism is an act of worship of the whole church. It should, therefore, ordinarily be administered in the context of corporate worship. If there are compelling reasons to administer the sacrament in some other context than the regular worship of a congregation, members of the congregation should still be present and scripture, proclamation, prayer and affirmation of the faith of the congregation should be a part of the act.

The meaning and significance of baptism are never limited to the person receiving the sacrament, but its benefits relate to all, as those present who have been baptized recall their own membership in the covenant community, the claim of God upon their own lives, and their dependence upon God's grace and forgiveness freely given.

The nature and character of baptism dictates that it can be administered only once to each person. The sign and seal once administered last for the whole course of our lives.

The proper recipients of baptism are believers and their children. The sacrament is to be administered by an ordained minister.

B. CELEBRATING THE SACRAMENT OF BAPTISM

It is recommended that prior to the celebration of the sacrament of baptism, the person to be baptized or the parent(s) of the child who is to be baptized should receive thorough instructions from the pastor and the session as to the meaning of baptism and its significance for the church and the one receiving the sacrament. After adequate instruction has been given, a date should be set for the celebration of the sacrament. The date should be a time when the regular worship of the congregation is anticipated.

The sacrament is administered during corporate worship in the context of affirmation of faith and may occur before or after the preaching of the Word. At the time in worship appointed for the sacrament, the minister may begin the celebration by simply asking that those who are to be baptized will come or be brought to the baptismal font. The minister, along with any others who are to assist in administering the sacrament, will then join them at the font. A hymn reflecting one of the themes of the sacrament may be sung.

Once at the font, with the participants in their proper places, the minister may then read or recite scripture passages which set forth the deep meaning of baptism found in scripture. Such texts as Isaiah 40:11; Acts 2:39; Matthew 28:18-19; Psalm 103:17-18, and Mark 10:15-16 are highly appropriate, as are many other texts.

The minister will then state for all to hear the meaning of baptism, emphasizing the notions of the covenant of grace, God's forgiveness of our sins, the outpouring of the Holy Spirit into our lives and declaring that through the sacrament we are marked as members of the household of faith.

The parents of those to be baptized, or each believer who is to be baptized, will next be asked to make affirmation of faith in Jesus Christ as their Lord and Savior, and they shall be asked to declare their willingness to be obedient to Christ through serving Christ as a member of Christ's church. Parents of children receiving baptism are also asked to declare their intention to teach their children of the love of God, to instruct them in the Christian faith, and to assist them to live lives obedient to the gospel.

The following questions and responses are suggestive of questions which could be used for the purposes stated above:

1. Who is your Lord and Savior?
   Jesus Christ is my Lord and Savior.
2. Do you trust in Jesus Christ for your salvation?
   I trust only in Jesus Christ.
3. Do you intend to be Christ's faithful disciple?
   I do so intend, with the help of the Holy Spirit.

The next two questions are to be asked only of the parent(s) of the children to be baptized:

4. Do you seek baptism for your child?
   I do, confessing its meaning for my salvation and the salvation of my child.
5. Do you intend to teach your child of the meaning of baptism for a person's life, the love of God and the meaning of Christian discipline?
   I so intend, relying greatly upon the Holy Spirit and the community of faith.

The members of the congregation are then to be asked if they will accept, witness to, and support the persons who are to be baptized, recognizing them as members of Christ's church. A question such as the following could be put to the worshiping congregation.

Do you, the people of God, members of Christ's church, promise to share with this new member the good news of the gospel, to surround (him/her) with love and compassion, and to support (him/her) through prayer, fellowship, and direction?

We do so promise and we so intend.

The response of the congregation being given, the minister will then lead the congregation in prayer, giving thanks for God's grace and forgiveness, God's love and mercy and for the church of Jesus Christ. Other biblical themes concerning baptism may be used to enrich the prayer. Moreover, it is in order to pray for the blessing of the water and the coming of the Holy Spirit into the life of the one to be baptized.

Following the prayer, the minister shall ask the Christian name of the one to be baptized. The congregation will then stand for the act of baptism.

Pouring or sprinkling water on the person who is to receive the sacrament the minister shall say:

"_____, I baptize you in the name of the Father and of the Son and of the Holy Spirit. Amen."

After the act of baptism the minister shall charge the congregation with respect to their responsibilities. A hymn may then be sung, or testimonies presented by members of the congregation. Or the minister may give witness to the fact that Christians are no longer aliens but fellow workers with Christ.

When persons being baptized are to be received into the church, the session may receive them before the act of baptism, or after the act of baptism, or at a meeting of the session at a later date.

Prayers may conclude the celebration, prayers of thanksgiving and intercession. The prayers may be in unison, silent or bidding in form. A blessing or peace may then be pronounced.

C. THE SACRAMENT OF THE LORD'S SUPPER AND CORPORATE WORSHIP

The sacrament of the Lord's Supper is not to be thought of as an addition to corporate worship; it is rather to be understood as central to Christian worship. It gives distinctive shape to the worship of Christians, and it should be celebrated frequently enough that it is clear to everyone that the Lord's Supper is a central part of corporate worship.

In the Lord's Supper God acts to give those who come to the table in faith the spiritual nourishment necessary to sustain them in their Christian lives. The quality and growth of one's life as a Christian are tied inseparably to this sacrament.

This sacrament is more than a memorial to, or a reminder of, Christ's sacrificial death and resurrection. It is a means, instituted by Christ for his disciples. through which the risen Lord is truly present with his people as a continuing power and reality. While the meaning of Christ's sacrificial death is at the heart of this sacrament, it is a resurrected, living Christ whom we encounter through the bread and the wine.

The time and place for each celebration of the Lord's Supper is to be set by the church judicatory which has jurisdiction over the group of Christians who are to celebrate the sacrament. The sacrament is to be offered freely to all who express personal faith, but all who are to partake were to be encouraged to confess their sins, to be reconciled to each other and to all human beings, and to come in humility and hope to Christ's table.

Celebrating the Lord's Supper

The sacrament of the Lord's Supper is to be celebrated as an integral part of corporate worship. Its administration will ordinarily follow the reading and proclamation of the word.

The celebration of the Lord's Supper may begin with the minister, or an elder authorized by the presbytery to administer the sacrament, reading or reciting scripture passages which speak of Christ's invitation to us to come to him. Matthew 11:28-30; Matthew 5:6; Luke 13:29; John 6:35, 48-51; John 10:10-11, and Revelation 3:20 are passages which may be used, but there are many others which may be used.

After the hymn has been sung the minister then reads or recites the biblical words of institution. These are passages of scripture which tell of Christ's institution of the Lord's Supper: I Corinthians 11:23-26; Luke 22:14-19; Matthew 26:26-28, and Mark 14:22-25.

The minister after presenting the words of institution then leads the worshipers in a prayer of thanksgiving. This prayer and its emphasis of thanksgiving has been so critical to this sacrament that the sacrament often is referred to as the Eucharist, which comes from the Greek word in the New Testament, *Eucharisto,* which means thanksgiving. It should include thanksgiving to God for the gift of Jesus Christ, thanksgiving for Christ's life, death and resurrection, and thanksgiving for Christ's presence among his people. Traditionally the prayer has also included a petition for the coming of the Holy Spirit to bring about our union with the risen Christ. It is appropriate that the Lord's Prayer follows the prayer of thanksgiving.

The minister may then break bread in the presence of the people, repeating the words of Jesus: "This is my body, which is for you; do this in remembrance of me."

The minister may then pour the wine in the presence of the people, voicing Jesus' words: "This cup is the new covenant in my blood. Do this, as often as you drink it, in remembrance of me."

It is in order for the minister and those assisting the minister themselves to partake of both elements, and then distribute the bread and wine to the other worshipers. As the elements are being passed, a hymn may be sung, or scripture may be read or silence observed.

As the minister gives the elements to the other worshipers, the minister may say: "This is the body of Christ; take, eat, and remember Christ died for your sins, and was raised victorious over sin and death."

and

"This is the blood of Christ; take, all of you drink of it, and remember that Christ died for your sins, and was raised victorious over sin and death."

or

"Jesus said: 'I am the bread of life, whoever comes to me will never be hungry; whoever believes in me will never thirst.'"

and

"Jesus said: 'I am the vine, you are the branches. Cut off from me you can do nothing.'"

When all the worshipers have been served, the minister may remind them of Christ's grace or bid them Christ's peace, using such phrases as: "The peace of God be with you" or "The grace of our Lord is yours."

The worshipers may then praise God by singing or reading a psalm, or by singing a hymn of praise.

It is proper that a brief prayer of praise and thanksgiving follow, after which a hymn may be sung. Following the hymn the worshipers may be given a charge and commissioned using such words as the following: "Go out into the world in peace and be the people of God; be of good courage; hold firmly to all that is good; return no person evil for evil; strengthen the fainthearted; support the weak; help those in need; treat all persons with respect and compassion; love and serve the Lord, rejoicing in the power of the Holy Spirit."

or

"Rejoice in the Lord always: Let all people know your gentleness and compassion and patience. Have no anxiety about anything, but in everything trust Christ who has promised to be with us always. And the peace of God keep your hearts and minds in Christ Jesus."

The service properly concludes with a blessing, after which the people may respond by saying:

"Alleluia! Amen!"

III. LITURGICAL RITES AND OCCASIONAL WORSHIP

A. PUBLIC PROFESSION OF FAITH

It is expected that corporate worship will be the occasion for persons to make public their professions of faith. This will be so for persons who are baptized as children of believing parents and also for persons who come to faith from outside the church. Both are reason for joy and rejoicing and for giving praise to God.

Such professions can appropriately take place in worship after the preaching of the gospel, and just prior to or as a part of the congregational affirmation of faith. Certainly professions of faith should be included in worship before the Lord's Supper is celebrated.

A variety of procedures may be used to incorporate into worship the personal profession of faith of individuals. An invitation to Christian discipleship may be extended following preaching of the gospel, and persons may present themselves to make public professions of faith at that time. Or groups of individuals who have received instruction may be presented to the congregation by the minister or a ruling elder. Again, sponsors may bring the persons forward and present them. Whatever procedure is used, it should honor the purpose and focus of worship; the procedure should never be seen as an interruption of worship or an intrusion into worship.

Once persons present themselves or are presented, they should be given the opportunity to profess their faith. Most often this is done according to the ancient custom in the church of asking questions. However, a congregation may give persons the opportunity of giving a statement of their personal faith in lieu of responding to questions.

When those making a public profession of faith desire to affiliate with the congregation, the following form of church covenant may be used:

1. Do you repent of your sin and believe Jesus Christ to be your Savior and the Lord of your life?
   I Do.
2. Do you believe the scriptures of the Old and New Testaments to be the inspired word of God, the source of authority for faith and practice, and will you read and study them for guidance in living the Christian life?
   I do so believe and I do so promise.
3. Do you promise to be a faithful member of this church by participating in worship, sharing in its ministry of witness and service, supporting the government of the Cumberland Presbyterian Church/Cumberland Presbyterian Church in America, and loving your brothers and sisters in Christ?
   I do so promise.
4. Will you strive to overcome temptation and weakness, grow in knowledge and grace, and practice love in all relationships,

being strengthened in your personal discipleship by your life in the community of faith?

I will so strive.

5. Do you promise to be a good steward of the life, talents, time, and money which God has entrusted to you, giving of these gifts to the church?

I do so promise.

An alternate form of church covenant which may be used is:

1. Who is your Lord and Savior?

Jesus Christ is my Lord and Savior.

2. Do you trust in Jesus Christ?

I do.

3. Do you intend to be Christ's disciple, to obey Christ's commands, and serve Christ?

I do, with the help of the Holy Spirit.

4. Do you intend to be a faithful member of the part of Christ's body called the Cumberland Presbyterian Church/Cumberland Presbyterian Church in America, worshiping and serving as a member of a local congregation, giving of yourself, your time and your substance?

I do so intend, relying upon God's grace.

After the questions have been answered, or the testimonies given, the minister shall acknowledge those professing their faith to be disciples of Jesus Christ, saying to each one something like the following:

"_____, you are a disciple of Jesus Christ. You are a fellow worker with us and with Christ. You are privileged to participate with all of Christ's disciples in Christ's redemptive work in the world."

A charge or commissioning may follow this declaration. Indeed, the minister may prepare a charge or commissioning statement for each occasion. The statements which follow may serve as a guide:

"Jesus said: 'As the Father has sent me, even so I send you.' Christ sends us into the world, as he was sent into the world, not to be ministered unto but to minister. May it be so for your life and for us all."

or

"Be filled with the Spirit of Christ. Live a life worthy of the gospel, with all lowliness and meekness, with patience, forbearing one another in love, eager to maintain the unity of the Spirit in the body of peace. Be an imitator of Christ. Walk in love."

After this charge, the church session may act to receive as members of the congregation those persons making a profession of faith. Or the session may act to receive them at a meeting soon thereafter. Then all present may join together in stating their common faith, using a traditional or contemporary creed.

Transfer of Membership or Reaffirmation of Faith

If persons who have previously made a public profession of faith desire to unite with a different congregation by transfer of membership or reaffirmation of faith, they may be acknowledged at this time. If they have already been received by the session, they may simply be introduced and recognized. If they have not yet been received they may be asked to declare their intentions publicly at this time and then be welcomed as members. An appropriate question would be:

Do you reaffirm your faith in Jesus Christ as your Lord and Savior, and do you transfer your membership and loyalty to this congregation?

I do, rejoicing in the opportunity to worship and serve God in this congregation.

After all individual professions of faith and declarations of intent have been stated, it is fitting that the session act to receive as members of that congregation all who have reaffirmed their faith. Or the session may act to receive them at a meeting soon thereafter. It is then highly appropriate that all present join together in an affirmation of faith, using one of the traditional or contemporary creeds of the church.

A prayer suitable for the occasion should follow, after which those who have been received as newly commissioned members are welcomed into the ministry of Jesus Christ to the community which the congregation serves.

B. CHRISTIAN MARRIAGE

Christian marriage is a relationship between a man and a woman in which they pledge their love to each other, commit themselves to one another, promise mutual fidelity and covenant to live together as husband and wife. Christians believe that God has ordained such a relationship for the welfare and happiness of humankind. While it is not necessary to be married to be an obedient Christian, and indeed not everyone should marry, it is in order for Christians to marry and to advocate marriage. Jesus Christ blessed the relationship of marriage, it has been honored in the church throughout the church's history, and it is to be held in high esteem among all people.

Marriage is a relationship recognized and defined by both the state and the church. The state views it as a civil contract among a woman and a man and the state with certain legal requirements placed upon all who enter into the civil contract. Moreover, the state requires that numerous requirements be met with respect to age, health and soundness of mind.

The church views marriage as more than a legal contract. Marriage is understood to be a relationship which is patterned after God's relationship to human beings in Jesus Christ. It involves self-giving, unselfish love one for the other and a profound sense of living their life together under the guidance and providential care of God.

Ministers are expected to counsel with a woman and a man who come to them to be married. That counseling will include instruction of the couple with respect to the biblical meaning of marriage, exploration of the commitment which the man and the woman have to each other, the requirements of the state, the design of the marriage service and the religious commitments of those who present themselves to be married.

Each minister will decide, based upon counseling with the couple, whether she or he can participate with the couple in the marriage ceremony. In making such a determination, the minister should consider matters such as the following: the concepts of marriage held by the couple, their commitment to Jesus Christ and the Christian church, their emotional, personal and financial suitability for marriage and their commitment to a marriage relationship. It is prudent for ministers at times to seek counsel from other ministers or laypersons in reaching a decision concerning his or her willingness to officiate at the marriage service of particular couples.

The Cumberland Presbyterian Church/Cumberland Presbyterian Church in America views a Christian service of marriage as a corporate worship experience. Consequently everything in principle which applies to corporate worship applies to a marriage service. The focus should be kept upon God and God's Word. All present are expected to participate. Indeed, it is highly appropriate for a man and a woman to be married as a part of a regular worship service. The man and the woman, as well as all members of the wedding party, engage in the scheduled corporate worship of the congregation, and come forward for the wedding service after the sermon and before the dismissal and/or benediction. It is also acceptable to have a service of marriage after the dismissal and/or benediction, with all members of the congregation invited to stay.

The essential elements of a marriage service are the following: (1) A brief statement of the meaning of Christian marriage by giving particular emphases to biblical material and themes. (2) Prayers for the couple as they enter into their new relationship. (3) An exchange of vows, appropriate to the Christian understanding of marriage between the woman and the man, and an exchange of rings if desired. (4) Scripture reading. (5) A charge delivered to the couple. (6) A public declaration that the man and woman are joined in marriage according to the ordinance of God and the law of the state. (7) The pronouncement of a blessing upon the couple.

The minister should provide counseling for the couple with respect to music. Any music which is a part of the Christian marriage ceremony should focus attention upon God, who sanctifies marriage. Hymns for congregation singing are recommended. If the minister lacks skill and knowledge in this area, it is highly recommended that counsel be sought from a competent, qualified musician.

Flowers, decorations and other appointments can add to the marriage service; however, care should be taken to avoid ostentation, excessive expense and that which is unduly elaborate.

At times a woman and man previously married in a civil ceremony may desire that their relationship be blessed by God through God's church. In such a situation, the minister will counsel with the couple, and if they demonstrate a Christian understanding of marriage and are genuinely seeking God's blessing on their marriage, then an appropriate service similar to a regular marriage ceremony may be performed as a part of a regularly scheduled service of corporate worship, or as a separate ceremony.

C. THE CHRISTIAN FUNERAL

Christians recognize the inevitability of death, and the Christian gospel powerfully addresses the reality and the experience of death. Christians are expected to affirm their confidence in Christ's victory over death and the grave and to proclaim that death cannot separate human beings from the love of God which is in Christ Jesus. Such is the faith by which Christians live and in which Christians die.

The belief of Christians in the resurrection from the dead is not a belief which denies the reality of death or suggests that persons have within them some form of immortality. Rather, it is a belief that God's love and power are greater than the power of death, so that though we die and cease to exist, we are given new life, a new existence in God's eternity. All this, Christians affirm because of the resurrection of Jesus Christ from the dead on the first day of the week.

The Christian community has special responsibilities toward

persons who are dying and toward those who are bereaved. Persons who are confronted with imminent death should not be isolated from the Christian community nor should members of the community try to convince them that they are not dying. Instead they should be supported with love, and affirmed as persons loved and forgiven by God.

When a person dies, the minister should be notified immediately. The minister, as well as others in the congregation, should go immediately to make contact with the family. It should be remembered that what is important on such an occasion is not what is said, but what is important is one's presence, and whom and what one represents. The minister should listen and be sensitive to the needs of those bereaved. It is expected that prayer will be offered with the family during the initial contact. If the minister of the congregation is not available, then one or more of the ruling elders should represent the church.

Ministers need to realize that the funeral is a cultural event as well as a religious event. Consequently ministers should be sensitive to customs regarding death and burial of the dead which are characteristic of each particular community and honor those customs whenever possible. This necessitates that ministers work creatively with funeral directors to ensure that there is adequate understanding on the part of the minister of various funeral practices and that there is an informal understanding of the funeral director with respect to the minister's theological understanding and practice.

The Christian funeral service is understood as a service of worship and should be approached as such. Thought should be given to the designing of the service, and it is expected that those present will participate in corporate worship. The singing of hymns, reading of scripture, preaching of the gospel, confession of sin, affirmation of faith, the celebration of the Lord's Supper are all appropriate to the Christian funeral service. In designing such a service, the family should be consulted and their desires should influence the shape and design of the service. It is strongly recommended that Christian funerals be conducted at the church. The casket shall be closed at all times during the service of worship.

It is not necessary to have the body of the deceased present for the service of worship which is occasioned by death. Services of worship with the body being absent are recognized as appropriate and equally meaningful as when a casket is present. Such a service may be scheduled before or after the committal service, if the body is to be interred.

The committal service should be performed with dignity and simplicity. It is to be brief, with scripture, prayer and a statement of the

Christian hope.

In all matters pertaining to the burial of the dead, ostentation, excessive expense, preoccupation with the cosmetic are to be avoided. The church is encouraged to support the wishes of the family of the bereaved with respect to memorial gifts in lieu of or in addition to flowers. At the church the use of a funeral pall is strongly recommended.

Christians have a responsibility to think through the different acceptable methods for disposing of the body of one who has died. Persons are urged to consider the matter long before death is imminent and make a decision with respect to the disposition of their bodies at the occasion of death. If the decision has not been made prior to one's death, the family should be assisted by the minister to examine the options. Interment, cremation and donation of the body for medical purposes are all Christian methods of disposing of the body.

D. INDIVIDUAL AND FAMILY WORSHIP

Individuals and families should order their lives so that time is available on a scheduled basis for prayer, reading of scripture, meditation and informed personal examination. They are to look to the church, particularly ordained ministers, for guidance and instruction in the nature, character and practice of prayer. All human beings need to be taught how to pray just as Jesus taught his disciples how to pray.

Family worship is also advocated to be practiced on a regular basis. In designing family worship, all members of the family should be considered, and worship should be designed so that all members can participate in the worship. Creativity and imagination are urged, and a variety of forms and approaches are desirable. Guidance from the church is to be sought.

It is important always for individuals and families to remember that their worship is to be regarded as a part of the worship of the church, the family of God. No Christian worship can ever be private worship; it is always a part of the worship of the great cloud of witnesses, living and dead, the universal church. One worships in the name of Jesus as a part of that church which is the body of Christ.

RULES OF ORDER

1.0 MODERATOR

1.1   The moderator has all the authority necessary to maintain order and for directing the business of the judicatory according to the rules and regulations of the church.

1.2   The minister in charge is the moderator of the session. The moderators of the other judicatories shall be elected for a set term and hold office until a successor is elected.

1.3   The moderator should be well-versed in parliamentary law and be familiar with the standing rules of the judicatory. At the same time, the moderator should bear in mind that rules are not a substitute for common sense.

1.4   It is the duty of the moderator:

a. to announce in proper sequence the business that comes before the judicatory in accordance with the agenda or program and the existing orders of the day;

b. to recognize members who are entitled to the floor;

c. to state and to put all questions that legitimately come before the judicatory as motions or that otherwise arise in the course of proceedings (except those that relate to the moderator), and to announce the result of each vote; or, if a motion that is not in order is made, to rule it out of order;

d. to protect the judicatory from frivolous or dilatory motions by refusing to recognize them;

e. to require that the rules relating to debate and to order and decorum within the judicatory be observed;

f. to expedite business in every way compatible with the rights of the members;

g. to decide all questions of order, subject to appeal--unless, when in doubt, such a question is submitted to the judicatory for decision;

h. to respond to inquiries of members relating to parliamentary procedure or factual information bearing upon the business of the judicatory;

i. to authenticate by signature, when necessary, all acts, orders, and proceedings of the judicatory;

j. to declare the meeting adjourned when the judicatory so votes or--when applicable--at the time prescribed on the program, or at any time in the event of a sudden emergency affecting the safety of those present:

k. to appoint all committees unless otherwise determined by the judicatory, and

l. to call the vice-moderator (or some other member) to the chair to preside temporarily; or before engaging in debate (except upon questions of order).

1.5 At each meeting, in addition to the necessary papers proper to that meeting's business, the moderator should have at hand:

a. a copy of the standing rules of the judicatory;

b. a copy of the *Rules of Order* of the Cumberland Presbyterian Church/Cumberland Presbyterian Church in America;

c. a copy of the current edition of *Robert's Rules of Order*, and

d. a memorandum of the complete order of business.

1.6 A judicatory may name the moderator an ex-officio member of all its boards and agencies (with voting rights); otherwise, the moderator is an advisory (non-voting) member of such boards and agencies.

1.7 If the moderator of a session is absent, or if the session is without a moderator, the clerk, or in his/her absence a member of the session, shall preside until a moderator pro tem is elected. In a congregation without a pastor, the moderator pro tem may be a member of the session or any ordained minister of the presbytery.

1.8 In judicatories above the session, if, during the term of office, the moderator is absent, the vice-moderator shall preside. If the vice-moderator is also absent (or if the judicatory does not have such an office), the stated clerk shall preside until a moderator pro tem is elected. In the absence of all of these officers, the members shall select a member of the judicatory to preside until a moderator pro tem is selected. If the absence occurs at the end of the moderator's term of office, the same procedure applies, but the member elected by the judicatory shall become the moderator, rather than the moderator pro tem.

1.9 When an issue is being considered by a judicatory that refers to the moderator in a capacity not shared in common with other members, or that commends or censures the moderator, the chair should be occupied by the vice-moderator or an appropriate temporary occupant.

2.0 VICE MODERATOR

2.1   A judicatory above the session may have a vice-moderator when such an office is incorporated within its standing rules which prescribe the manner of election.

2.2   The vice-moderator shall perform the duties of the moderator during the absence or disability of the moderator or in the case of a vacancy in the office of moderator, and shall perform such other duties as from time to time may be assigned to the office of vice-moderator by the judicatory.

3.0 STATED CLERK

3.1   Each judicatory shall elect a stated clerk who shall preserve all minutes, documents, and papers committed to the office of stated clerk and submit these records to the next higher judicatory in compliance with that judicatory's rules and regulations.

3.2   The stated clerk shall be elected for a definite term (normally three years) and shall hold office until a successor is elected.

3.3   All records and documents are the property of the judicatory and shall be kept and stored in accordance with the provision of the Constitution. Upon leaving office, the stated clerk shall transfer all such records and documents to the successor.

3.4   It shall be the duty of the stated clerk to record all minutes in permanent form and to supply extracts from them when properly requested. The stated clerk shall perform the duties of the office of stated clerk during the meeting of the judicatory unless otherwise determined by the judicatory. Other duties of the stated clerk shall be:

a. to keep on file all committee records;
b. to keep the judicatory's official membership roll;
c. to make copies of the official minutes of the judicatory and distribute them to the members prior to the next stated meeting (unless otherwise determined by the judicatory);
d. to notify officers, committee members and delegates of their election or appointment, to furnish committees with whatever documents are required for the performance of their duties and to have on hand at each meeting a list of all existing committees and their members;
e. to certify delegates or commissioners;
f. to sign the minutes of all meetings;
g. to read all papers to be acted upon (unless otherwise determined

by the judicatory), and

h. to record any vote which requires more than a majority following a polling of the judicatory or a division of the house.

3.5 The stated clerk shall record only those motions which are adopted unless instructed otherwise by the judicatory.

3.6 The stated clerk may or may not be a member of the judicatory.

4.0 TREASURER

4.1 The treasurer shall be elected for a definite period of time (normally a three-year term).

4.2 The treasurer shall keep the books properly posted so as to be able to provide a current report on the financial condition of the judicatory.

4.3 The treasurer shall prepare a detailed annual report at the end of each fiscal year and such supplemental reports as the judicatory may require.

4.4 The treasurer shall present the financial records for an annual review or audit, the nature of such to be determined by the judicatory.

4.5 The treasurer shall not disburse any funds without proper authorization from the judicatory.

4.6 The treasurer may or may not be a member of the judicatory.

5.0 OPENING AND CLOSING OF JUDICATORY MEETINGS

5.1 The moderator shall open the meetings at the appointed time by taking the chair, calling the meeting to order, and after ascertaining that a quorum is present, calling the judicatory to prayer.

5.2 Should a quorum not be present at the appointed time, any two members can adjourn the meeting from time to time to afford an opportunity for a quorum to convene.

5.3 Following the roll call, the minutes not previously approved shall be read, corrected, and approved by a vote of the judicatory. The minutes of a church session shall be corrected and approved at the close of the meeting or at the beginning of the next regular meeting. The minutes of all judicatories above the church session shall be corrected and approved before the adjournment of that particular meeting. If the existence of an error or material omission in the minutes becomes reasonably established after their approval--even many years later-- the minutes can then be corrected by means of the motion to *Amend Something Previously Adopted*, which requires unanimous consent or a two-thirds vote.

5.4   The moderator of every judicatory above the session, in closing its meeting, may have a hymn to be sung in addition to the praying of a closing prayer or the pronouncement of a benediction.

6.0 QUORUMS

6.1   A majority of the session shall constitute a quorum unless the congregation has set a quorum otherwise.

6.2   Four members shall constitute a quorum for the presbytery provided at least one minister and one elder are present.

6.3   Six members from at least three presbyteries shall constitute a quorum for synod providing this includes at least one minister and one elder.

6.4   Any twenty or more commissioners, of whom at least ten are ministers and ten elders shall constitute a quorum for the General Assembly.

7.0 ADOPTION OF PROGRAM: ORDERS OF THE DAY

7.1   A program or agenda is adopted by a majority vote and is always subject to change. However, after having been adopted, a two-thirds vote is required for change.

7.2   An order of the day is a particular subject, question, or item of business that is set in advance to be taken up at a given session, day, or meeting, or at a given hour provided that no business having precedence over it interferes.

7.3   Orders of the day are divided into two classes: general orders and special orders. When an hour is assigned to a particular subject on the program, that subject is thereby made a special order. Subjects for which no hour is specified are general orders.

7.4   An order of the day that has been set for a particular hour cannot be considered before that hour unless the rules are suspended by a two-thirds vote.

7.5   A general order cannot be considered if other business is pending or if a prior general order has not been considered. A special order interrupts all business except certain privileged questions (See *Robert's Rules of Order*).

7.6   Regular order of business:
a. Reading and Approval of Minutes (session only)
b. Reading and Referring (or acting upon) Communications Addressed to the Judiciary
c. Reading of Resolutions
d. Reports of Officers, Boards, Standing Committees and

Commissions
e. Reports of Select Committees
f. Unfinished Business
g. New Business

8.00 MOTIONS

8.10 Bringing a Motion Before a Judicatory

8.11 There are three steps by which a motion is normally brought before a judicatory: (1) a member makes a motion; (2) another member seconds the motion, and (3) the moderator states the question on the motion.

8.12 To make a motion a member must rise, address the moderator and be recognized, and then state the motion.

8.13 The purpose of a second is to assure that more than one member of the judicatory wants to deal with a particular issue. It is not necessary for a member to obtain the floor to second a motion. A motion made by direction of a committee composed of judicatory members requires no second from the floor.

8.20 Considering a Motion

8.21 There are three basic steps by which a motion is considered:
a. the members debate the motion (if debatable);
b. the moderator puts the question (has the members vote), and
c. the moderator announces the result of the vote.

8.30 Types of Motions

8.31 Main Motion

Purpose: To bring business before the judicatory.

Characteristics: Requires a second; is debatable; is amendable; requires only a majority vote (with few exceptions, see *Robert's Rules of Order*); can be reconsidered.

8.32 Subsidiary Motions

Purpose: To assist the judicatory in treating or dispensing of main motions.

A listing of subsidiary motions from the lowest to the highest in the order of precedence:
a. Postpone Indefinitely

Purpose: To kill a main motion for the duration of the session and avoid a direct vote on the question.

Characteristics: Requires a second; is debatable; is not amendable; requires only a majority vote; an affirmative vote can be reconsidered, a negative vote cannot.

b. Amend

Purpose: To modify the wording--and within certain limits (see *Robert's Rules of Order*, Section 12) the meaning--of a pending motion.

Characteristics: Requires a second; is debatable; is generally amendable; requires only a majority vote; can be reconsidered.

c. Commit or Refer

Purpose: To send a pending question to a committee so that the question may be carefully investigated and put into better condition for the judicatory to consider.

Characteristics: Requires a second; is debatable; is amendable; requires only a majority vote; can be reconsidered if the committee has not begun consideration of the question.

d. Postpone to a Certain Time (or Definitely)

Purpose: To defer action on a pending question within limits (see *Robert's Rules of Order*, section 14) to a definite day, meeting, or hour, or until after a certain event.

Characteristics: Requires a second; is debatable; is amendable; requires only a majority vote; can be reconsidered.

e. Limit or Extend the Limits of Debate

Purpose: To exercise special control over debate.

Characteristics: Requires a second; is not debatable; is amendable but any amendment is undebatable; requires a two-thirds vote; can be reconsidered without debate any time before the order limiting or extending debate is exhausted.

f. Previous Question

Purpose: To bring the judicatory to an immediate vote on one or more pending questions.

Characteristics: Requires a second; is not debatable; is not amendable (except another member can move the previous question on more or fewer pending questions); requires a two-thirds vote; can be reconsidered (before any vote has been taken).

g. Lay on the Table

Purpose: To allow the judicatory to lay the pending question aside temporarily.

Characteristics: Requires a second; is not debatable; is not amendable; requires only a majority vote; cannot be reconsidered.

8.33   Privileged Motions

Purpose: To allow the judicatory, without debate, to deal with special matters of immediate and overriding importance that do not relate to the pending business.

A listing of privileged motions from the lowest to the highest in the order of precedence:

a. Call for the Orders of the Day
Purpose: To require the judicatory to follow its adopted program or agenda.
Characteristics: Does not require a second; is not debatable; is not amendable; does not require a vote, but can be set aside by a two-thirds vote; cannot be reconsidered.

b. Raise a Question of Privilege
Purpose: To permit a request or main motion relating to the rights and privileges of the judicatory or any of its members to be brought up for immediate consideration while business is pending.
Characteristics: Does not require a second; is not debatable; is not amendable; is ruled upon by the moderator; cannot be reconsidered.

c. Recess
Purpose: To permit a short intermission in the judicatory's proceedings which does not close the meeting, and after which business will be immediately resumed at the point where it was interrupted.
Characteristics: Requires a second; is not debatable; is amendable as to the length of time, but such an amendment is not debatable; requires only a majority vote; cannot be reconsidered.

d. Adjourn
Purpose: To close the present meeting when no time for adjourning has been set and provision for a future meeting exists.
Characteristics: Requires a second; is not debatable; is not amendable; requires only a majority vote; cannot be reconsidered.

e. Fix Time to Which to Adjourn
Purpose: To set the time, and sometimes the place, for another meeting to continue business of the session with no effect on when the present meeting will adjourn.
Characteristics: Requires a second; is not debatable; is amendable as to the date, hour or place, but such amendments are not debatable; requires only a majority vote; can be reconsidered.

8.34   Incidental Motions
Purpose: To raise incidental questions (usually questions of procedure).   Incidental questions usually must be decided before business can proceed.
A listing of incidental motions:

a. Point of Order
Purpose: To call upon the moderator for a ruling and an enforcement of the rules of order.
Characteristics: Does not require a second; is not debatable; is not amendable; is ruled upon by the chair (no vote is taken unless the

moderator is in doubt or his ruling is appealed); cannot be reconsidered.

b. Appeal

Purpose: To take the moderator's ruling to the judicatory for final decision.

Characteristics: Requires a second; is normally undebatable (see *Robert's Rules of Order* for exceptions); is not amendable; a majority or tie vote sustains the decision of the moderator; can be reconsidered.

c. Suspend the Rules

Purpose: To allow the judicatory to do something it cannot do without violating one or more of its regular rules.

Characteristics: Requires a second; is not debatable; is not amendable; requires a two-thirds vote; cannot be reconsidered.

d. Objection to the Consideration of a Question

Purpose: To enable the judicatory to avoid a particular main motion when it believes it would be undesirable for the motion to even come before the judicatory.

Characteristics: Does not require a second; is not debatable; is not amendable; a two-thirds vote against consideration is required to sustain the objection; a vote sustaining the objection can be reconsidered, but one not sustaining the objection cannot.

e. Division of a Question

Purpose: To allow the parts of a question to be separated.

Procedure: The motion to divide must clearly state the manner in which the question is to be divided. A motion cannot be divided unless each part presents a proper question for the judicatory to act upon if none of the other parts are adopted. If a series of independent questions are offered in one motion, the questions must receive separate consideration at the request of a single member and the motion for Division of a Question is not used. (See *Robert's Rules of Order*, Section 27).

Characteristics: Requires a second; is not debatable; is amendable; requires only a majority vote; cannot be reconsidered.

f. Consideration by Paragraph or Seriatim

Purpose: To allow a report or long motion consisting of a series of resolutions, paragraphs, articles, or sections to be considered by opening the different parts to debate and amendment separately.

Procedure: Each sub-division should be read, explained by its proponent and then opened for debate and amendment. Amendments are voted on as they arise, but no sub-division is finally adopted at that time. After all parts have been considered, the entire document is opened for amendment. Following this, the vote is taken on the entire document as amended.

Characteristics: Requires a second; is not debatable; is amendable; requires only a majority vote; cannot be reconsidered.

g. Division of the Judiciary

Purpose: To allow a member, whenever that member doubts the results of a voice vote, or a vote by show of hands, or that a representative number of the members present have voted, to require a standing vote.

Characteristics: Does not require a second; is not debatable; is not amendable; does not require a vote since a single member can demand a division; cannot be reconsidered.

8.35   Motions that Bring a Question Again Before the Judicatory

Purpose: To allow the judicatory to bring questions before it again through special procedures.

A list of motions that bring questions again before the judicatory:

a. Take from the Table

Purpose: To bring before the judicatory a motion or a series of adhering motions that has previously been laid on the table.

Characteristics: Requires a second; is not debatable; is not amendable; requires only a majority vote; cannot be reconsidered but can be renewed each time that any business has been transacted.

b. Rescind; Amend something previously Adopted (two forms of one motion)

Purpose: To allow a previous action or order to be canceled or countermanded. The form to Rescind should be used when the object is to delete; the form to Amend Something Previously Adopted should be used when the object is to change a portion or all of a text.

Characteristics: Require a second; are debatable; are amendable; require a two-thirds vote, a negative vote can be reconsidered, but an affirmative cannot. These motions are not in order when it has previously been moved to reconsider the vote on the main motion, and the question can be reached by calling up the motion to Reconsider. There is no time limit on these matters and they can be moved by any member, regardless of how the member voted on the original question.

To Expunge: It shall require the unanimous vote of the members present to expunge any matter from the records.

c. Discharge a Committee

Purpose: To take a matter out of a committee's hands before the committee has made a final report on it. So long as a question is in the hands of a committee, the judicatory cannot consider another motion involving practically the same question.

Characteristics: Requires a second; is debatable; is amendable; requires a two-thirds vote; a negative vote can be reconsidered, but not an affirmative vote.

d. Reconsider

Purpose: To allow the judicatory--within a limited time and without notice--to bring back for further consideration a motion which has already been voted on.

Characteristics: Requires a second; is debatable when the original question was debatable; is not amendable; requires only a majority vote regardless of the vote necessary to adopt the motion to be considered; cannot be reconsidered.

Special requirements of this motion:

i. It can only be made by a member who voted with the prevailing side.

ii. In a meeting of more than one day, the motion to reconsider can be moved only on the same day the original vote was taken, or on the next succeeding day.

8.40 Miscellaneous Rules Concerning Motions

a. Until the moderator states the question, the maker has the right to modify the motion or to withdraw it.

b. After the question has been stated by the moderator, the motion becomes property of the judicatory and cannot be modified or withdrawn without the judicatory's consent.

c. If the maker of a motion modifies it before the question is stated, the member who seconded it has a right to withdraw the second.

9.00 AMENDMENTS

9.10 Classification as to form

9.11   To insert or to add words or a paragraph.

9.12   To strike out words or a paragraph.

9.13   To strike out and insert (which applies to words) or to substitute (which applies to one or more paragraphs).

9.20 To Amend by Substitution

9.21   A motion to amend by striking out one or more paragraphs and adding one or more new paragraphs as a replacement is called a motion to substitute. In the case of a motion to substitute, the pending question is first opened to improvement by secondary amendment; then opportunity is given to amend the proposed substitute--so that both the pending question and the substitute may be put in the most desirable form before the vote is taken on whether the substitution shall be made. If the motion to substitute is carried, the substituted material can no longer be amended except by adding nonmodifying matter.

9.30 Primary and Secondary Amendments

9.31   A primary amendment amends a main motion. A secondary amendment amends a primary amendment. (It is sometimes called an amendment to the amendment). A secondary amendment cannot be amended since it would make parliamentary procedure too complicated.

9.40 Improper Amendments

9.41   Improper amendments include those that:
a. are not germane to the question to be amended;
b. merely make the adoption of the amended question equivalent to a rejection of the amended motion;
c. purposes to change one form of an amendment to another, and
d. would have the effect of converting one parliamentary motion into another.

10.00 ASSIGNMENT OF THE FLOOR AND DEBATE

10.01   To gain the floor, a member must rise, address the moderator, and be recognized by the moderator.

10.02   If two or more members rise to seek the floor at the same time, the one farthest from the moderator shall be recognized.

10.03   Until a matter has been brought before the judicatory in the form of a motion proposing a specific action, it cannot be debated.

10.04   A member having obtained the floor for the purpose of engaging in debate can speak no longer than ten minutes without obtaining the consent of the judicatory. Such permission can be given by unanimous consent or by means of a motion to extend the limits of debate which requires a two-thirds vote and is not debatable.

10.05   No member can speak more than twice to the same question on the same day without the consent of the judicatory. Asking or answering a question is not counted as speaking in debate.

10.06   Debate can be closed by moving the previous question. The previous question can be applied to any pending debatable or amendable motion; to an entire series of such motions; or to any consecutive part of such a series.

10.07 Rights in debate are not transferrable. A member may not yield a portion of time to another member or reserve it for later except by unanimous consent or by suspension of the rules.

10.08 In debate a member's remarks must be germane to the question before the judicatory. For example, when a secondary amendment is the pending question, the member can debate only that amendment, not the primary amendment or the main motion.

10.09 When a question is pending, that measure can be criticized in strong terms, but personalities should not be brought into the debate nor should the motives of other members be questioned or attacked. Members should always treat one another with respect.

10.10 Members of the judicatory should not address one another directly, but should address all remarks through the moderator.

10.11 As much as possible, the use of members' names should be avoided in debate.

11.0 NOMINATIONS AND ELECTIONS

11.1 Nominations are usually made by a nominating committee and from the floor. The use of a nominating committee must not preclude the making of nominations from the floor.

11.2 A nominating committee should be elected by the judicatory unless its composition is determined by the standing rules.

11.3 Whenever possible, a member's consent should be obtained before that member's name is placed in nomination.

11.4 After a motion to close nominations is duly made and seconded, two votes must be taken: the first, to close nominations; the second, to elect the nominees.

11.5 Election to an office becomes final immediately, if the candidate is present, and does not decline; or if absent, has given prior consent. If the member is absent and has not given prior consent, the election becomes final when notice of election is given to the member, provided the member does not immediately decline.

11.6 A judicatory after having elected one of its members to represent it at a higher judicatory shall not instruct that member how to vote on the issues; however, counseling with representatives is always in order.

12.0 VOTING

12.1   Voting is normally by voice, by rising, by show of hands, or by ballot.

12.2   When more than one person is nominated for the same office, the method of voting shall be by ballot.

12.3   All members who are eligible to vote shall do so unless excused by the judicatory. Members thus excused shall not be allowed a vote in subsequent proceedings relating to that particular question.

12.4   The moderator shall vote only when the moderator's vote would create or break a tie, or cause or block the attainment of a two-thirds majority, or when the vote is taken by roll call.

12.5   No member of a judicatory shall participate in debate or vote on a matter in which the member has a pecuniary interest, a personal interest, or other conflict of interest not common to other members of the judicatory. A member of a judicatory has such a conflict of interest when the member also belongs to a lower judicatory whose action is the subject of an appeal to or review by the higher judicatory. In such a case, the member may participate as a representative of the lower judicatory but may not participate as a member of the higher judicatory. Members are not prevented from voting for themselves for an office or other or other position to which members generally are eligible (see *Robert's Rules of Order*, Section 45).

12.6   When various motions are made with respect to the filling of blanks with particular numbers or times, the question shall always be first taken on the highest number and the longest time.

12.7   When the moderator has begun taking the vote, no further debate or remark shall be allowed except to correct a mistake.

12.8   A roll call vote on any question shall not be taken unless requested by at least one-fifth of the members present.

12.9   In all elections, a majority of votes are necessary to elect.

13.00 BOARDS, COMMITTEES AND COMMISSIONS

13.01   A board is an administrative body of elected persons whose powers are delegated to it by the authority of the judicatory.

13.02   A board cannot delegate its authority, but any board can appoint subcommittees to work under its supervision or according to its specific instructions. Such subcommittees always report to the board.

13.03   A committee is a body of one or more persons, elected or appointed by a judicatory to consider, investigate, or take action on certain matters or subjects, or to do all of these things.

13.04 Committees are of two types: standing committees (which have a continuing existence) and special committees (which go out of existence as soon as they have completed a specified task or tasks). Special committees are sometimes called select committees or ad hoc committees.

13.05 The first person named on a committee shall be considered the chairperson, whose duties it shall be to convene the committee and preside over its meetings. If for any reason this person cannot act in this capacity, the second person named shall assume these responsibilities.

13.06 The moderator shall appoint the usual standing committees but shall not raise new committees without instruction.

13.07 A member who is in opposition to the whole matter upon which a committee is to act shall not be compelled to serve on that committee.

13.08 A committee has less authority to act independently for the judicatory than a board. When a judicatory needs an ad hoc group, which can act with more authority than a committee normally has, a commission should be elected. Commissions differ from ordinary committees in that while a committee can simply examine, consider and report, a commission is authorized to deliberate upon and conclude the business submitted to it, subject to the review of the judicatory appointing it.

13.09 Board reports which are reviewed by a select committee cannot be amended by the judicatory and, if printed, shall be printed as submitted by the board. However, board reports which are brought directly to the floor of the judicatory for review and action shall be treated as committee reports and be subject to amendment, but the judicatory shall not make such a board report (or a committee or commission report) appear to say something different from the wording that was actually reported. For this reason, the published report would show clearly whatever changes the judicatory makes by the use of brackets, underlining, italics, or other appropriate means.

13.10 A judicatory may accept a report by concurring in it and adopting its recommendations, or by simply adopting its recommendations.

13.11 No action apart from filing is necessary upon a report that contains only statements of fact or opinions for judicatory information.

13.12 Minority reports shall be heard only by consent of, or by a majority vote of, the judicatory. When a minority report is presented it is for information only and it cannot be acted upon except by a motion to substitute it for the report of the committee.

13.13 Ex-officio members of boards and committees are members by virtue of some office that they hold. There is no distinction between ex-officio members and appointed or elected members. When ex-officio members cease to hold the offices that entitle them to membership on a board or committee, their membership terminates automatically.

13.14 Advisory members are non-voting members who have the privilege of offering counsel or advice to the board or committee.

13.15 Members of judicatory boards and committees who are not members of the judicatory may vote in the board and committee meetings but not in the meetings of the judicatory.

13.16 Every judicatory has a right to resolve itself into a Committee of the Whole, in which members may freely converse together without the formalities necessary in their ordinary proceedings. In all such cases the moderator shall name the member who is to preside as chairperson. If the committee be unable to agree, a motion may be made that the committee rise; and upon adoption of such motion, the moderator shall resume the chair, and the chairperson of the committee shall report what has been done, and ask that the committee be discharged, which being allowed, the matter shall be dropped. If the committee shall agree upon the report to be made, or have made progress in the same without coming to a conclusion, the committee may rise, report what has been done, and, if the case require, may ask leave to sit again; or the Committee of the Whole may be dissolved, and the question considered by the judicatory in the usual order of business.

14.0 CASES NOT PROVIDED FOR IN THESE RULES

14.1   These Rules of Order are based on *Robert's Rules of Order.* All cases that may arise which are not provided for in these Rules or in the Government of the church shall be governed by *Robert's Rules of Order.*